Note

AS WITH MANY of the plays of William Shakespeare (1564–1616), the dating of *Antony and Cleopatra* can at best be guessed. The Stationers' Register for May 20, 1608, contains an entry for "A booke Called Anthony. and Cleopatra" and for another called "Pericles prynce of Tyre," also one of Shakespeare's subjects: neither was immediately published, and it is likely that their entry was an effort to block the publication of pirated versions of the two plays. In 1607 Samuel Daniel published a revised edition of his *Tragedie of Cleopatra* (1593), his alterations showing a familiarity with Shakespeare's tragedy. It may safely be assumed, therefore, that *Antony and Cleopatra* was composed and staged in late 1606 or early 1607, following soon after *King Lear* and *Macbeth*.

Shakespeare already had treated the political life of Ancient Rome— in *Julius Cæsar* (1599)—but his decision to continue the story of Mark Antony may in fact be due to that character's proven popularity with Tudor and Elizabethan audiences. If Daniel had revised his *Cleopatra* to capitalize on the other's success, Shakespeare himself knew and was indebted to his predecessor's version. It is likely that he had also read *Antonius*, the Countess of Pembroke's translation of Garnier's *Marc Antoine*, and that he remembered the portrait of Antony in Spenser's *Faerie Queen*, previously a source for *King Lear*. And there is no doubt that Shakespeare knew almost by heart Thomas North's *Lives of the noble Grecians and Romanes* (1579), the translation of a French edition of Plutarch's *Parallel Lives* from which he also took elements of *Julius Cæsar*, *A Midsummer Night's Dream*, and *Coriolanus*.

Antony and Cleopatra remains largely faithful to North's version of Plutarch, in both story and language. Shakespeare is vague about the amount of time encompassed by the play (about ten years: the lapse between Antony's death and that of Cleopatra was of months, not hours as Shakespeare maintains), and he glosses over such details as Antony's three children by Octavia, but the play's action on the whole transpires in the order given by Plutarch. Indeed, many of the most memorable incidents and descriptions in Shakespeare's play have their foundation in the other writer's work, from the fabulous tales of Cleopatra's tricks and Antony's debauches, to the very wording of certain passages: compare, for example, Enobarbus's report of Antony and Cleopatra's first meeting (II, ii) with the following lines form North:

> She disdained to set forward otherwise, but to take her barge in the river of Cydnus, the poope whereof was of gold, the sailes of purple, and the owers of silver, which kept stroke in rowing after the sounde of the musicke of flutes, howboyes, citherns, violls, and such other instruments as they played upon in the barge. And now for the person of her self: she was layed under a pavillion of cloth of gold of tissue, apparelled and attired like the goddesse Venus, commonly drawen in picture: and hard by her, on either hand of her, pretie faire boyes apparelled as painters doe set forth god Cupide, with litle fannes in their hands, with the which they fanned wind upon her . . .

Nowhere else is the playwright's source so discernible through his words.

Shakespeare's indebtedness to North's Plutarch, however, is limited to the language and plot of the play, for his interpretation of the lovers' story is decidedly different. The older writer, a Greek who lived for some time in Rome, admires Antony but treats him as Cleopatra's victim, an instance of Roman virtue brought down by Eastern sensuality: "the horse of the minde . . . that is so hard of rayne (I meane the unreyned lust of concupiscence) did put out of Antonius heade, all honest and commendable thoughtes." Shakespeare, however, counterbalances the Roman view with that of Egypt. To him, the couple resemble nothing so much as a more experienced, middle-aged Romeo and Juliet, ennobled rather than diminished by the love that proves their undoing. Certainly Cleopatra is a vain and selfish woman who toys with Antony — at the cost of his life — to the last, but there is little doubt that her emotion is real, her passion felt. And Antony, once thought to have been "transform'd Into a strumpet's fool," his duties as a ruler neglected in the pursuit of pleasure, restores his nobility by choosing to die for love. As Cæsar himself forecasts in the play's closing lines, though Rome is triumphant, its victory will be equaled if not eclipsed in fame by the tragedy of Egypt.

DOVER · THRIFT · EDITIONS

Antony and Cleopatra

WILLIAM SHAKESPEARE

Lepidus — (about him)

1. 4   too indulgent
11. 7   huge sphere
11. 7   I am not so well as I should be
11. 7   These quicksands, L,/keep off them
                                    for you sink
III. 2 Agrippa + Enobarbus ridicule him
"II. 5 'the poor third is up' + 'fool Lepidus'
III. 6 'Lepidus was grown too cruel.

DOVER PUBLICATIONS, INC.
Mineola, New York

DOVER THRIFT EDITIONS

GENERAL EDITOR: PAUL NEGRI
EDITOR OF THIS VOLUME: ADAM FROST

Copyright

Published in Canada by General Publishing Company, Ltd., 30 Lesmill Road, Don Mills, Toronto, Ontario.

Published in the United Kingdom by Constable and Company, Ltd., 3 The Lanchesters, 162–164 Fulham Palace Road, London W6 9ER.

Theatrical Rights

Bibliographical Note

This Dover edition, first published in 1998, contains the unabridged text of *Antony and Cleopatra* as published in Volume XVIII of *The Caxton Edition of the Complete Works of William Shakespeare*, Caxton Publishing Company, London, n.d. The Note was prepared specially for this edition, and explanatory footnotes from the Caxton edition have been supplemented and revised.

Library of Congress Cataloging-in-Publication Data

Shakespeare, William, 1564–1616.
　　Antony and Cleopatra / William Shakespeare.
　　　　p.　cm. — (Dover thrift editions)
　　ISBN 0-486-40062-X (pbk.)
　　1. Antonius, Marcus, 83?–30 B.C.—Drama. 2. Cleopatra, Queen of Egypt, d. 30 B.C.—Drama. 3. Rome—History—Civil War, 43–31 B.C.—Drama. I. Title. II. Series.
PR2802.A1　1998
822.3'3—DC21　　　　　　　　　　　　　　　　　　　　　　　　97-32464
　　　　　　　　　　　　　　　　　　　　　　　　　　　　　　　　　CIP

Manufactured in the United States of America
Dover Publications, Inc., 31 East 2nd Street, Mineola, N.Y. 11501

Contents

Fortune.

Dramatis Personæ

ANTONY,
OCTAVIUS CÆSAR, } triumvirs.
LEPIDUS,

SEXTUS POMPEIUS.

DOMITIUS ENOBARBUS,
VENTIDIUS,
EROS,
SCARUS, } friends to Antony.
DERCETAS,
DEMETRIUS,
PHILO,

MÆCENAS,
AGRIPPA,
DOLABELLA,
PROCULEIUS, } friends to Cæsar.
THYREUS,
GALLUS,

MENAS,
MENECRATES, } friends to Sextus Pompeius.
VARRIUS,

TAURUS, lieutenant-general to Cæsar.

CANIDIUS, lieutenant-general to Antony.

SILIUS, an officer in Ventidius's army.

EUPHRONIUS, an ambassador from Antony to Cæsar.

ALEXAS,
MARDIAN, a eunuch, } attendants on Cleopatra.
SELEUCUS,
DIOMEDES,

A Soothsayer.
A Clown.

CLEOPATRA, queen of Egypt.
OCTAVIA, sister to Cæsar, and wife to Antony.
CHARMIAN, } attendants on Cleopatra.
IRAS,

Officers, Soldiers, Messengers, and other Attendants.

SCENE: *In several parts of the Roman empire*

ACT I.

SCENE I. *Alexandria. A Room in Cleopatra's Palace.*

Enter DEMETRIUS *and* PHILO

PHILO.   Nay, but this dotage of our general's
    O'erflows the measure: those his goodly eyes,
    That o'er the files and musters of the war
    Have glow'd like plated[1] Mars, now bend, now turn,
    The office and devotion of their view
    Upon a tawny front: his captain's heart,
    Which in the scuffles of great fights hath burst
    The buckles on his breast, reneges all temper,[2]
    And is become the bellows and the fan
    To cool a gipsy's lust.

Flourish. Enter ANTONY, CLEOPATRA, *her Ladies, the Train, with*
Eunuchs *fanning her*

                Look, where they come:
    Take but good note, and you shall see in him
    The triple pillar[3] of the world transform'd
    Into a strumpet's fool: behold and see.
CLEO.   If it be love indeed, tell me how much.
ANT.   There's beggary in the love that can be reckon'd.
CLEO.   I'll set a bourn[4] how far to be beloved.
ANT.   Then must thou needs find out new heaven, new earth.

Enter an Attendant

ATT.   News, my good lord, from Rome.
ANT.   Grates me: the sum.[5]

---

1. *plated*] armor-clad.
2. *reneges all temper*] renounces all self-restraint.
3. *The triple pillar*] the third pillar. Antony was one of the triumvirs, Octavius and
    Lepidus being the other two.
4. *bourn*] boundary, limit.
5. *Grates me: the sum*] This vexes me; be brief.

1

CLEO. Nay, hear them,[6] Antony:
　　　Fulvia perchance is angry; or, who knows
　　　If the scarce-bearded Cæsar have not sent
　　　His powerful mandate to you, "Do this, or this;
　　　Take in that kingdom, and enfranchise that;
　　　Perform 't, or else we damn thee."

ANT.　　　　　　　　　　　How, my love!

CLEO. Perchance! nay, and most like:
　　　You must not stay here longer, your dismission
　　　Is come from Cæsar; therefore hear it, Antony.
　　　Where's Fulvia's process?[7] Cæsar's I would say? both?
　　　Call in the messengers. As I am Egypt's queen,
　　　Thou blushest, Antony, and that blood of thine
　　　Is Cæsar's homager:[8] else so thy cheek pays shame
　　　When shrill-tongued Fulvia scolds. The messengers!

ANT. Let Rome in Tiber melt, and the wide arch
　　　Of the ranged[9] empire fall! Here is my space.
　　　Kingdoms are clay: our dungy earth alike
　　　Feeds beast as man: the nobleness of life
　　　Is to do thus; when such a mutual pair　　　　　[*Embracing.*
　　　And such a twain can do 't, in which I bind,
　　　On pain of punishment, the world to weet[10]
　　　We stand up peerless.

CLEO.　　　　　　　Excellent falsehood!
　　　Why did he marry Fulvia, and not love her?
　　　I'll seem the fool I am not; Antony
　　　Will be himself.[11]

ANT.　　　　　　But stirr'd by Cleopatra.
　　　Now, for the love of Love and her soft hours,
　　　Let's not confound the time with conference harsh:
　　　There's not a minute of our lives should stretch
　　　Without some pleasure now. What sport to-night?

CLEO. Hear the ambassadors.

---

6. *them*] the news (in plural).
7. *process*] summons.
8. *homager*] vassal.
9. *ranged*] well-ordered, well built.
10. *to weet*] to know.
11. *I'll seem . . . be himself*] Cleopatra means that in giving herself up to Antony she is
　　not so foolish as to ignore his faithlessness to his wife, Fulvia. Antony will yet dis-
　　cover his faithless character and forsake his new love.

[handwritten: Egypt has been hard to conquer]

ANT.   Fie, wrangling queen!
  Whom every thing becomes, to chide, to laugh,
  To weep; whose every passion fully strives
  To make itself, in thee, fair and admired!
  No messenger but thine; and all alone
  To-night we'll wander through the streets and note *[handwritten: — historical Plutarch]*
  The qualities of people. Come, my queen;
  Last night you did desire it. Speak not to us.
                     [*Exeunt Ant. and Cleo. with their train.*

DEM.   Is Cæsar with Antonius prized so slight? *[handwritten: — nothing like the Antony]*
PHI.   Sir, sometimes, when he is not Antony,
  He comes too short of that great property
  Which still should go with Antony.
DEM.   I am full sorry
  That he approves[12] the common liar, who *[handwritten: what is being said about him]*
  Thus speaks of him at Rome: but I will hope
  Of better deeds to-morrow. Rest you happy! [*Exeunt.*

SCENE II. *The Same. Another Room.*

Enter CHARMIAN, IRAS, ALEXAS, *and a* Soothsayer

CHAR.   Lord Alexas, sweet Alexas, most any thing Alexas, almost most
     absolute Alexas, where's the soothsayer that you praised so to the
     queen? O, that I knew this husband, which, you say, must charge
     his horns with garlands![1]
ALEX.   Soothsayer!
SOOTH.   Your will?
CHAR.   Is this the man? Is't you, sir, that know things?
SOOTH.   In nature's infinite book of secrecy
     A little I can read.
ALEX.   Show him your hand.

---

12. *approves*] corroborates.

---

1. *must charge . . . garlands*] must wear the signs of conjugal dishonor as though they
   were a desirable ornament.

Enter ENOBARBUS

ENO.   Bring in the banquet quickly; wine enough
      Cleopatra's health to drink.

CHAR.   Good sir, give me good fortune.

SOOTH.   I make not, but foresee.

CHAR.   Pray then, foresee me one.

SOOTH.   You shall be yet far fairer than you are.

CHAR.   He means in flesh.

IRAS.   No, you shall paint when you are old.

CHAR.   Wrinkles forbid!

ALEX.   Vex not his prescience; be attentive.

CHAR.   Hush!

SOOTH.   You shall be more beloving then beloved.

CHAR.   I had rather heat my liver[2] with drinking.

ALEX.   Nay, hear him.

CHAR.   Good now, some excellent fortune! Let me be married to three
      kings in a forenoon, and widow them all: let me have a child at
      fifty, to whom Herod of Jewry[3] may do homage: find me to marry
      me with Octavius Cæsar, and companion me with my mistress.

SOOTH.   You shall outlive the lady whom you serve.

CHAR.   O excellent! I love long life better than figs.

SOOTH.   You have seen and proved a fairer former fortune
      Than that which is to approach.

CHAR.   Then belike my children shall have no names:[4] prithee, how
      many boys and wenches must I have?

SOOTH.   If every of your wishes had a womb,
      And fertile every wish, a million.

CHAR.   Out, fool! I forgive thee for a witch.[5]

ALEX.   You think none but your sheets are privy to your wishes.

CHAR.   Nay, come, tell Iras hers.

ALEX.   We'll know all our fortunes.

ENO.   Mine and most of our fortunes to-night shall be—drunk to bed.

IRAS.   There's a palm presages chastity, if nothing else.

CHAR.   E'en as the o'erflowing Nilus presageth famine.

IRAS.   Go, you wild bedfellow, you cannot soothsay.

---

2. *liver*] The liver was held to be the seat of love.

3. *Herod of Jewry*] the biblical tyrant who ordered the slaughter of the children of
    Judæa (*Matthew* 2:1–18).

4. *shall have no names*] shall be illegitimate.

5. *for a witch*] because you are a wizard.

CHAR.   Nay, if an oily palm[6] be not a fruitful prognostication, I cannot
 scratch mine ear.[7] Prithee, tell her but a worky-day[8] fortune.

SOOTH.   Your fortunes are alike.

IRAS.   But how, but how? give me particulars.

SOOTH.   I have said.

IRAS.   Am I not an inch of fortune better than she?

CHAR.   Well, if you were but an inch of fortune better than I, where
 would you choose it?

IRAS.   Not in my husband's nose.

CHAR.   Our worser thoughts heavens mend! Alexas,—come, his fortune, his fortune! O, let him marry a woman that cannot go, sweet
 Isis, I beseech thee! and let her die too, and give him a worse! and
 let worse follow worse, till the worst of all follow him laughing to
 his grave, fifty-fold a cuckold! Good Isis, hear me this prayer,
 though thou deny me a matter of more weight; good Isis, I beseech thee!

IRAS.   Amen. Dear goddess, hear that prayer of the people! for, as it is
 a heart-breaking to see a handsome man loose-wived, so it is a
 deadly sorrow to behold a foul knave uncuckolded: therefore, dear
 Isis, keep decorum, and fortune him accordingly!

CHAR.   Amen.

ALEX.   Lo, now, if it lay in their hands to make me a cuckold, they
 would make themselves whores, but they'ld do't!

ENO.   Hush! here comes Antony.

CHAR.   Not he; the queen.   *one + the same*

Enter CLEOPATRA

CLEO.   Saw you my lord?

ENO.   No, lady.

CLEO.   Was he not here?

CHAR.   No, madam.

CLEO.   He was disposed to mirth; but on the sudden
 A Roman thought hath struck him. Enobarbus!

ENO.   Madam?

CLEO.   Seek him, and bring him hither. Where's Alexas?

ALEX.   Here, at your service. My lord approaches.

CLEO.   We will not look upon him: go with us.   [*Exeunt.*

---

6. *an oily palm*] a sweaty palm, indicating a lustful disposition.
7. *I cannot scratch mine ear*] I am a helpless fool; a proverbial phrase.
8. *worky-day*] work-a-day, ordinary.

Enter ANTONY *with a* Messenger *and* Attendants

MESS.   Fulvia thy wife first came into the field.
ANT.   Against my brother Lucius?
MESS.   Ay:
     But soon that war had end, and the time's state
     Made friends of them, jointing⁹ their force 'gainst Cæsar,
     Whose better issue in the war from Italy
     Upon the first encounter drave them.
ANT.   Well, what worst?
MESS.   The nature of bad news infects the teller.
ANT.   When it concerns the fool or coward. On:
     Things that are past are done with me. 'T is thus;
     Who tells me true, though in his tale lie death,
     I hear him as he flatter'd.
MESS.   Labienus—
     This is stiff news—hath with his Parthian force
     Extended¹⁰ Asia from Euphrates,
     His conquering banner shook from Syria
     To Lydia and to Ionia,
     Whilst—
ANT.   Antony, thou wouldst say,—
MESS.   O, my lord!
ANT.   Speak to me home,¹¹ mince not the general tongue:
     Name Cleopatra as she is call'd in Rome;
     Rail thou in Fulvia's phrase, and taunt my faults
     With such full license as both truth and malice
     Have power to utter. O, then we bring forth weeds
     When our quick minds lie still, and our ills told us
     Is as our earing.¹² Fare thee well awhile.
MESS.   At your noble pleasure.   [*Exit.*
ANT.   From Sicyon, ho, the news! Speak there!
FIRST ATT.   The man from Sicyon, is there such an one?
SEC. ATT.   He stays upon your will.
ANT.   Let him appear.

---

  9. *jointing*] uniting.
10. *Extended*] seized upon; a legal phrase.
11. *home*] directly, without mincing words.
12. *O, then we bring forth . . . our earing*] The meaning is "just as the plough stirs up
      the soil of land run to weeds, so does the declaration of our sinfulness improve our
      minds when immersed in sloth and luxury."

These strong Egyptian fetters I must break,
Or lose myself in dotage.

Enter another Messenger

                    What are you?
SEC. MESS.   Fulvia thy wife is dead.
ANT.   Where died she?
SEC. MESS.   In Sicyon:
Her length of sickness, with what else more serious
Importeth thee to know, this bears.   [*Gives a letter.*
ANT.   Forbear me.[13]
                                [*Exit Sec. Messenger.*
There's a great spirit gone! Thus did I desire it:
What our contempts do often hurl from us,
We wish it ours again; the present pleasure,
By revolution lowering,[14] does become
The opposite of itself: she's good, being gone;
The hand could pluck[15] her back that shoved her on.
I must from this enchanting queen break off:
Ten thousand harms, more than the ills I know,
My idleness doth hatch. How now! Enobarbus!

Re-enter ENOBARBUS

ENO.   What's your pleasure, sir?
ANT.   I must with haste from hence.
ENO.   Why then we kill all our women. We see how mortal an un-
kindness is to them; if they suffer our departure, death's the word.
ANT.   I must be gone.
ENO.   Under a compelling occasion let women die: it were pity to cast
them away for nothing; though, between them and a great cause,
they should be esteemed nothing. Cleopatra, catching but the
least noise of this, dies instantly; I have seen her die twenty times
upon far poorer moment:[16] I do think there is mettle in death,
which commits some loving act upon her, she hath such a celerity in dying.
ANT.   She is cunning past man's thought.

13. *Forbear me*] Leave my presence.
14. *By revolution lowering*] growing worse by the turning of fortune's wheel.
15. *could pluck*] would willingly pluck.
16. *upon far poorer moment*] for far less reason.

ENO.   Alack, sir, no; her passions are made of nothing but the finest part of pure love: we cannot call her winds and waters sighs and tears; they are greater storms and tempests than almanacs can report: this cannot be cunning in her; if it be, she makes a shower of rain as well as Jove.

ANT.   Would I had never seen her!

ENO.   O, sir, you had then left unseen a wonderful piece of work; which not to have been blest withal would have discredited your travel.

ANT.   Fulvia is dead.

ENO.   Sir?

ANT.   Fulvia is dead.

ENO.   Fulvia!

ANT.   Dead.

a good thing

ENO.   Why, sir, give the gods a thankful sacrifice. When it pleaseth their deities to take the wife of a man from him, it shows to man the tailors of the earth, comforting therein, that when old robes are worn out there are members to make new. If there were no more women but Fulvia, then had you indeed a cut, and the case to be lamented: this grief is crowned with consolation; your old smock brings forth a new petticoat: and indeed the tears live in an onion that should water this sorrow.   (pretence)

ANT.   The business she hath broached in the state
    Cannot endure my absence.

ENO.   And the business you have broached here cannot be without you; especially that of Cleopatra's, which wholly depends on your abode.

ANT.   No more light answers. Let our officers
    Have notice what we purpose. I shall break
    The cause of our expedience[17] to the queen
    And get her leave to part. For not alone
    The death of Fulvia, with more urgent touches,[18]
    Do strongly speak to us, but the letters too
    Of many our contriving friends in Rome
    Petition us at home: Sextus Pompeius[19]
    Hath given the dare to Cæsar and commands
    The empire of the sea: our slippery people,

political

17. *expedience*] hasty departure.
18. *urgent touches*] pressing motives.
19. *Sextus Pompeius*] Pompey the Great's son, now a rival to Cæsar.

Whose love is never link'd to the deserver
Till his deserts are past, begin to throw
Pompey the Great and all his dignities
Upon[20] his son; who, high in name and power,
Higher than both in blood and life, stands up
For the main[21] soldier: whose quality, going on,
The sides o' the world may danger. Much is breeding,
Which, like the courser's hair,[22] hath yet but life
And not a serpent's poison. Say, our pleasure,
To such whose place is under us, requires
Our quick remove from hence.

ENO.   I shall do 't.   [*Exeunt.*

SCENE III. *The Same. Another Room.*

Cleopatra's trickery is part of her power (politically + sexually)

Enter CLEOPATRA, CHARMIAN, IRAS, *and* ALEXAS

CLEO.   Where is he?
CHAR.   I did not see him since.
CLEO.   See where he is, who's with him, what he does:
        I did not send you: if you find him sad,
        Say I am dancing; if in mirth, report
        That I am sudden sick: quick, and return.   [*Exit Alexas.*
CHAR.   Madam, methinks, if you did love him dearly
        You do not hold the method to enforce
        The like from him.
CLEO.   What should I do, I do not?
CHAR.   In each thing give him way, cross him in nothing.
CLEO.   Thou teachest like a fool: the way to lose him.
CHAR.   Tempt him not so too far; I wish, forbear:
        In time we hate that which we often fear.
        But here comes Antony.

20. *throw . . . Upon*] bestow . . . upon.
21. *main*] principal, pre-eminent.
22. *the courser's hair*] horse's hair, which was popularly believed to turn into a poison-
    ous serpent if laid in water.

Enter ANTONY

CLEO.   I am sick and sullen. *— give hands*

ANT.   I am sorry to give breathing to my purpose,—

CLEO.   Help me away, dear Charmian; I shall fall:
It cannot be thus long, the sides of nature
Will not sustain it.

ANT.   Now, my dearest queen,— *goes to Cleo.*

CLEO.   Pray you, stand farther from me.

ANT.   What's the matter?

CLEO.   I know, by that same eye, there's some good news.
What says the married woman? You may go:
Would she had never given you leave to come!
Let her not say 'tis I that keep you here,
I have no power upon you; hers you are.

ANT.   The gods best know—

CLEO.   O, never was there queen   *— sit down*
So mightily betray'd! yet at the first
I saw the treasons planted.

ANT.   Cleopatra,—

CLEO.   Why should I think you can be mine and true,
Though you in swearing shake the throned gods,
Who have been false to Fulvia? Riotous madness,
To be entangled with those mouth-made vows,
Which break themselves in swearing!

ANT.   Most sweet queen,— *move t*
                                              Cleo

CLEO.   Nay, pray you, seek no colour[1] for your going,
But bid farewell, and go: when you sued staying,
rises / Then was the time for words: no going then;
from   Eternity was in our lips and eyes,
chair   Bliss in our brows' bent, none our parts so poor *to audience*
         But was a race[2] of heaven: they are so still,
Or thou, the greatest soldier of the world,
Art turn'd the greatest liar.

ANT.   How now, lady!

CLEO.   I would I had thy inches; thou shouldst know
There were a heart in Egypt.

ANT.   Hear me, queen:

1. *colour*] pretext, pretence.
2. *a race*] a smack or flavor.

The strong necessity of time commands
Our services awhile; but my full heart
Remains in use[3] with you. Our Italy
Shines o'er with civil swords: Sextus Pompeius
Makes his approaches to the port of Rome:
Equality of two domestic powers
Breed scrupulous[4] faction: the hated, grown to strength,
Are newly grown to love: the condemn'd Pompey,
Rich in his father's honour, creeps apace
Into the hearts of such as have not thrived
Upon the present state, whose numbers threaten;
And quietness grown sick of rest would purge
By any desperate change. My more particular,
And that which most with you should safe[5] my going,
Is Fulvia's death.

CLEO.   Though age from folly could not give me freedom,
It does from childishness: can Fulvia die?

ANT.   She's dead, my queen:
Look here, and at thy sovereign leisure read
The garboils[6] she awaked: at the last, best;
See when and where she died.

CLEO.   O most false love!
Where be the sacred vials[7] thou shouldst fill
With sorrowful water? Now I see, I see,
In Fulvia's death, how mine received shall be.

ANT.   Quarrel no more, but be prepared to know
The purposes I bear, which are, or cease,
As you shall give the advice. By the fire
That quickens Nilus' slime, I go from hence
Thy soldier, servant, making peace or war
As thou affect'st.

CLEO.   Cut my lace, Charmian, come;
But let it be: I am quickly ill and well,
So Antony loves.

ANT.   My precious queen, forbear;

3. *in use*] in pledge, in usufruct.
4. *scrupulous*] captious.
5. *safe*] render safe.
6. *garboils*] tumults, commotions.
7. *sacred vials*] the bottles filled with tears of kinsfolk, supposedly placed by Romans in the tombs of the departed.

And give true evidence to his love, which stands
An honourable trial.

CLEO.   So Fulvia told me.
I prithee, turn aside and weep for her;
Then bid adieu to me, and say the tears
Belong to Egypt:[8] good now, play one scene
Of excellent dissembling, and let it look
Like perfect honour.

ANT.   You'll heat my blood: no more.

CLEO.   You can do better yet; but this is meetly.[9]

ANT.   Now, by my sword,—

CLEO.   And target. Still he mends;
But this is not the best. Look, prithee, Charmian,
How this Herculean Roman[10] does become
The carriage of his chafe.[11]

ANT.   I'll leave you, lady.

CLEO.   Courteous lord, one word.
Sir, you and I must part, but that's not it:
Sir, you and I have loved, but there's not it:
That you know well: something it is I would,—
O, my oblivion is a very Antony,
And I am all forgotten.[12]

ANT.   But that your royalty
Holds idleness your subject, I should take you
For idleness itself.

CLEO.   'T is sweating labour
To bear such idleness so near the heart
As Cleopatra this. But, sir, forgive me,
Since my becomings kill me when they do not
Eye well to you. Your honour calls you hence;
Therefore be deaf to my unpitied folly,
And all the gods go with you! Upon your sword
Sit laurel victory! and smooth success
Be strew'd before your feet!

ANT.   Let us go. Come;

---

8. *Belong to Egypt*] belong to the Queen of Egypt.
9. *meetly*] pretty fair.
10. *this Herculean Roman*] Antony claimed descent from Anton, son of Hercules.
11. *does become . . . his chafe*] is ennobled by his angry mien.
12. *O, my oblivion . . . forgotten*] O, my forgetful memory is deserting me, just like Antony himself, and I have lost memory of everything.

Our separation so abides and flies,
That thou residing here go'st yet with me,
And I hence fleeting here remain with thee.
Away!   [*Exeunt.*

SCENE IV. *Rome. Cæsar's House.*

Enter OCTAVIUS CÆSAR, *reading a letter,* LEPIDUS, *and their train*

CÆS.   You may see, Lepidus, and henceforth know,
        It is not Cæsar's natural vice to hate
        Our great competitor: from Alexandria
        This is the news: he fishes, drinks and wastes
        The lamps of night in revel: is not more manlike
        Than Cleopatra, nor the queen of Ptolemy
        More womanly than he: hardly gave audience, or
        Vouchsafed to think he had partners: you shall find there
        A man who is the abstract[1] of all faults
        That all men follow.
LEP.   I must not think there are
        Evils enow to darken all his goodness:
        His faults in him seem as the spots of heaven,
        More fiery by night's blackness, hereditary
        Rather than purchased, what he cannot change
        Than what he chooses.
CÆS.   You are too indulgent. Let us grant it is not
        Amiss to tumble on the bed of Ptolemy,
        To give a kingdom for a mirth, to sit
        And keep the turn of[2] tippling with a slave,
        To reel the streets at noon and stand the buffet
        With knaves that smell of sweat: say this becomes him,—
        As his composure must be rare indeed
        Whom these things cannot blemish,—yet must Antony
        No way excuse his soils, when we do bear

---

1. *abstract*] epitome.
2. *keep . . . of*] take turns.

So great weight in his lightness. If he fill'd
His vacancy with his voluptuousness,
Full surfeits and the dryness of his bones
Call on him[3] for 't: but to confound such time
That drums him from his sport and speaks as loud
As his own state and ours, 't is to be chid
As we rate boys, who, being mature in knowledge,
Pawn their experience to their present pleasure,
And so rebel to judgement.

Enter a Messenger

Lep.   Here 's more news.
Mess.   Thy biddings have been done; and every hour,
Most noble Cæsar, shalt thou have report
How 't is abroad. Pompey is strong at sea;
And it appears he is beloved of those
That only have fear'd Cæsar:[4] to the ports
The discontents repair, and men's reports
Give him much wrong'd.

Military + political change.

Cæs.   I should have known no less:
It hath been taught us from the primal state,
That he which is was wish'd until he were;
And the ebb'd man, ne'er loved till ne'er worth love,
Comes dear'd by being lack'd. This common body,
Like to a vagabond flag[5] upon the stream,
Goes to and back, lackeying[6] the varying tide,
To rot itself with motion.

} — Sea imagery

Mess.   Cæsar, I bring thee word,
Menecrates and Menas, famous pirates,
Make the sea serve them, which they ear[7] and wound
With keels of every kind: many hot inroads
They make in Italy; the borders maritime
Lack blood to think on 't, and flush youth revolt:[8]
No vessel can peep forth, but 't is as soon

---

3. *Call on him*] Call him to account.
4. *fear'd Cæsar*] adhered to Cæsar from fear, not love.
5. *a vagabond flag*] a floating rush or reed.
6. *lackeying*] dancing attendance on like a lackey.
7. *ear*] plough.
8. *Lack blood . . . revolt*] turn pale at the thought of it, and youth in the first flush of
manhood rises in rebellion.

Taken as seen; for Pompey's name strikes more
Than could his war resisted.

CÆS.   Antony,
Leave thy lascivious wassails. When thou once
Wast beaten from Modena, where thou slew'st
Hirtius and Pansa, consuls, at thy heel
Did famine follow; whom thou fought'st against,
Though daintily brought up, with patience more
Than savages could suffer: thou didst drink
The stale of horses and the gilded puddle
Which beasts would cough at: thy palate then did deign
The roughest berry on the rudest hedge;
Yea, like the stag, when snow the pasture sheets,
The barks of trees thou browsedst. On the Alps
It is reported thou didst eat strange flesh,
Which some did die to look on: and all this—
It wounds thine honour that I speak it now—
Was borne so like a soldier that thy cheek
So much as lank'd⁹ not.

LEP.   'T is pity of him.

CÆS.   Let his shames quickly
Drive him to Rome: 't is time we twain
Did show ourselves i' the field; and to that end
Assemble we immediate council: Pompey
Thrives in our idleness.

LEP.   To-morrow, Cæsar,
I shall be furnish'd to inform you rightly
Both what by sea and land I can be able
To front¹⁰ this present time.

CÆS.   Till which encounter,
It is my business too. Farewell.

LEP.   Farewell, my lord: what you shall know meantime
Of stirs abroad, I shall beseech you, sir,
To let me be partaker.

CÆS.   Doubt not, sir;
I knew it for my bond.¹¹   [Exeunt.

---

9. *lank'd*] shrank, showed lankness.
10. *To front*] in order to meet.
11. *I knew it for my bond*] I regarded it as my bounden duty.

SCENE V. *Alexandria. Cleopatra's Palace.*

Enter CLEOPATRA, CHARMIAN, IRAS, *and* MARDIAN

CLEO.   Charmian!
CHAR.   Madam?
CLEO.   Ha, ha!
   Give me to drink mandragora.[1]
CHAR.   Why, madam?
CLEO.   That I might sleep out this great gap of time
   My Antony is away.
CHAR.   You think of him too much.
CLEO.   O, 'tis treason!
CHAR.   Madam, I trust, not so.
CLEO.   Thou, eunuch Mardian!
MAR.   What's your highness' pleasure?
CLEO.   Not now to hear thee sing; I take no pleasure
   In aught an eunuch has: 'tis well for thee,
   That, being unseminar'd,[2] thy freer thoughts
   May not fly forth of Egypt. Hast thou affections?
MAR.   Yes, gracious madam.
CLEO.   Indeed!
MAR.   Not in deed, madam; for I can do nothing
   But what indeed is honest to be done:
   Yet have I fierce affections, and think
   What Venus did with Mars.
CLEO.   O Charmian,
   Where think'st thou he is now? Stands he, or sits he?
   Or does he walk? or is he on his horse?
   O happy horse, to bear the weight of Antony!   *sexual.*
   Do bravely, horse! for wot'st thou whom thou movest?
   The demi-Atlas of this earth, the arm
   And burgonet[3] of men. He's speaking now,
   Or murmuring "Where's my serpent of old Nile?"   *portent of*
   For so he calls me: now I feed myself   *ending*
   With most delicious poison. Think on me,

---

1. *mandragora*] an herb, of which the infusion was a powerful opiate.
2. *unseminar'd*] emasculated.
3. *burgonet*] helmet.

That am with Phœbus' amorous pinches black
And wrinkled deep in time? Broad-fronted Cæsar,
When thou wast here above the ground, I was
A morsel for a monarch: and great Pompey[4]
Would stand and make his eyes grow in my brow;
There would he anchor his aspect and die
With looking on his life.

Enter ALEXAS

ALEX.   Sovereign of Egypt, hail!
CLEO.   How much unlike art thou Mark Antony!
   Yet, coming from him, that great medicine hath   *To have been*
   With his tinct[5] gilded thee.   *near him*
   How goes it with my brave Mark Antony?
ALEX.   Last thing he did, dear queen,
   He kiss'd—the last of many doubled kisses—
   This orient pearl. His speech sticks in my heart.
CLEO.   Mine ear must pluck it thence.
ALEX.   "Good friend," quoth he,
quotation   "Say, the firm Roman to great Egypt sends
   This treasure of an oyster; at whose foot,
   To mend the petty present, I will piece
   Her opulent throne with kingdoms; all the east,   *— promises*
   Say thou, shall call her mistress." So he nodded,
   And soberly did mount an arm-gaunt[6] steed,
   Who neigh'd so high, that what I would have spoke
   Was beastly dumb'd[7] by him.
CLEO.   What, was he sad or merry?
ALEX.   Like to the time o' the year between the extremes
   Of hot and cold, he was nor sad nor merry.
CLEO.   O well divided disposition! Note him,
   Note him, good Charmian, 'tis the man; but note him:
   He was not sad, for he would shine on those
   That make their looks by his; he was not merry,

---

4. *great Pompey*] Cneius (or Gnaeus) Pompeius, son of Pompey the Great, is referred
   to.
5. *tinct*] tincture, the grand elixir of the alchemists, thought to turn base metal into
   gold.
6. *arm-gaunt*] variously defined as "gaunt from long service in war," "high-spirited,"
   and "caparisoned in armor or warlike equipment."
7. *beastly dumb'd*] was made inaudible by the beast's neighs.

Which seem'd to tell them his remembrance lay
In Egypt with his joy; but between both.
O heavenly mingle![8] Be'st thou sad or merry,
The violence of either thee becomes,
So does it no man else. Met'st thou my posts?

ALEX.   Ay, madam, twenty several messengers:
Why do you send so thick?

CLEO.   Who's born that day
When I forget to send to Antony,
Shall die a beggar. Ink and paper, Charmian.
Welcome, my good Alexas. Did I, Charmian,
Ever love Cæsar so?

CHAR.   O that brave Cæsar!

CLEO.   Be choked with such another emphasis!
Say, the brave Antony.

CHAR.   The valiant Cæsar!

CLEO.   By Isis, I will give thee bloody teeth,   *incomparable lov*
If thou with Cæsar paragon[9] again
My man of men.

CHAR.   By your most gracious pardon,
I sing but after you.

CLEO.   My salad days,
When I was green in judgement: cold in blood,
To say as I said then! But come, away;
Get me ink and paper:
He shall have every day a several greeting,
Or I'll unpeople Egypt.   [*Exeunt.*

8. *mingle*] combination.
9. *paragon*] compare or parallel.

ACT II.

Scene I. *Messina. Pompey's House.*

Enter Pompey, Menecrates, *and* Menas, *in warlike manner*

POMPEY.   If the great gods be just, they shall assist
　　The deeds of justest men.
MENE.　　　　　　　　Know, worthy Pompey,
　　That what they do delay, they not deny.
POM.   Whiles we are suitors to their throne, decays
　　The thing we sue for.
MENE.　　　　　　We, ignorant of ourselves,
　　Beg often our own harms, which the wise powers
　　Deny us for our good; so find we profit
　　By losing of our prayers.
POM.　　　　　　　I shall do well:
　　The people love me, and the sea is mine;
　　My powers are crescent,[1] and my auguring hope
　　Says it will come to the full. Mark Antony
　　In Egypt sits at dinner, and will make
　　No wars without doors: Cæsar gets money where
　　He loses hearts: Lepidus flatters both,
　　Of both is flatter'd, but he neither loves,
　　Nor either cares for him.
MEN.　　　　　　　　Cæsar and Lepidus
　　Are in the field: a mighty strength they carry.
POM.   Where have you this? 'tis false.
MEN.　　　　　　　　From Silvius, sir.
POM.   He dreams: I know they are in Rome together,
　　Looking for Antony. But all the charms of love,
　　Salt[2] Cleopatra, soften thy waned[3] lip!
　　Let witchcraft join with beauty, lust with both!
　　Tie up the libertine in a field of feasts,

*shows
— knowledge
of individua[l]*

---

1. *crescent*] growing.
2. *Salt*] wanton, lustful.
3. *waned*] faded.

19

Keep his brain fuming; Epicurean cooks
Sharpen with cloyless sauce his appetite;
That sleep and feeding may prorogue[4] his honour
Even till a Lethe'd dulness!

Enter VARRIUS

                    How now, Varrius!
VAR.   This is most certain that I shall deliver:
     Mark Antony is every hour in Rome
     Expected: since he went from Egypt 't is
     A space for farther travel.[5]
POM.   I could have given less matter
     A better ear. Menas, I did not think
     This amorous surfeiter would have donn'd his helm
     For such a petty war: his soldiership
     Is twice the other twain: but let us rear
     The higher our opinion, that our stirring
     Can from the lap of Egypt's widow[6] pluck
     The ne'er-lust-wearied Antony.
MEN.   I cannot hope[7]
     Cæsar and Antony shall well greet together:
     His wife that's dead did trespasses to Cæsar;
     His brother warr'd upon him; although, I think,
     Not moved by Antony.
POM.   I know not, Menas,
     How lesser enmities may give way to greater.
     Were 't not that we stand up against them all,
     'T were pregnant they should square between themselves;[8]
     For they have entertained cause enough
     To draw their swords: but how the fear of us
     May cement their divisions and bind up
     The petty difference, we yet not know.
     Be 't as our gods will have 't! It only stands

---

4. *prorogue*] to keep in a languishing state.
5. A *space for farther travel*] A space of time has elapsed for a longer journey than that from Egypt to Rome.
6. *Egypt's widow*] Cleopatra had been married to her brother Ptolemy at the instance of Julius Cæsar.
7. *hope*] expect.
8. *'T were pregnant . . . themselves*] It were likely that they should quarrel amongst themselves.

Our lives upon to use[9] our strongest hands.
Come, Menas.   [*Exeunt.*

SCENE II. *Rome. The House of Lepidus.*

Enter ENOBARBUS *and* LEPIDUS

LEP.   Good Enobarbus, 'tis a worthy deed,
   And shall become you well, to entreat your captain
   To soft and gentle speech.

[handwritten note: Trying to ease the way]

ENO.   I shall entreat him
   To answer like himself: if Cæsar move him,
   Let Antony look over Cæsar's head
   And speak as loud as Mars. By Jupiter,
   Were I the wearer of Antonius' beard,
   I would not shave 't[1] to-day.

[handwritten note: There will be conflict between A + Cae.]

LEP.   'Tis not a time
   For private stomaching.[2]
ENO.   Every time
   Serves for the matter that is then born in 't.
LEP.   But small to greater matters must give way.
ENO.   Not if the small come first.
LEP.   Your speech is passion:
   But, pray you, stir no embers up. Here comes
   The noble Antony.

Enter ANTONY *and* VENTIDIUS

ENO.   And yonder, Cæsar.

Enter CÆSAR, MÆCENAS, *and* AGRIPPA

ANT.   If we compose well here, to Parthia:
Hark, Ventidius.

9. *It only stands . . . to use*] our lives wholly depend upon our using.

---

1. *I would not shave 't*] Since plucking the beard was a symbolic act for starting a fight,
   the speaker implies that, were he Antony, he would not avoid a conflict with Cæsar.
2. *stomaching*] quarreling.

A stiff and 'arcling' meeting.

CÆS.   I do not know,
    Mæcenas; ask Agrippa.
LEP.   Noble friends,
    That which combined us was most great, and let not
    A leaner action rend us. What's amiss,
    May it be gently heard: when we debate
    Our trivial difference loud, we do commit
    Murder in healing wounds: then, noble partners,
    The rather for I earnestly beseech,
    Touch you the sourest points with sweetest terms,
    Nor curstness grow to the matter.[3]
ANT.   'T is spoken well.
    Were we before our armies and to fight,
    I should do thus.   [*Flourish.*
CÆS.   Welcome to Rome.
ANT.   Thank you.
CÆS.   Sit.
ANT.   Sit, sir.
CÆS.   Nay, then.
ANT.   I learn, you take things ill which are not so,
    Or being, concern you not.
CÆS.   I must be laugh'd at,
    If, or for nothing or a little, I
    Should say myself[4] offended, and with you
    Chiefly i' the world; more laugh'd at, that I should
    Once name you derogately,[5] when to sound your name
    It not concern'd me.
ANT.   My being in Egypt, Cæsar,
    What was't to you?
CÆS.   No more than my residing here at Rome
    Might be to you in Egypt: yet, if you there
    Did practise on my state,[6] your being in Egypt
    Might be my question.
ANT.   How intend you, practised?
CÆS.   You may be pleased to catch at mine intent

---

3. *Nor curstness grow to the matter*] nor let ill-humored speech be added to the real sub-
    ject of our difference.
4. *say myself*] declare myself.
5. *derogately*] disparagingly.
6. *practise on my state*] conspire against my position.

By what did here befal me. Your wife and brother
Made wars upon me, and their contestation
Was theme for you,[7] <u>you were the word of war.</u>

ANT.   You do mistake your business; my brother never
Did urge me in his act:[8] I did inquire it,
And have my learning from some true reports
That drew their swords with you. Did he not rather
Discredit my authority with yours,
And make the wars alike against my <u>stomach,</u>
Having alike your cause? Of this my letters
Before did satisfy you. If you'll patch[9] a quarrel,
As matter whole you have not to make it with,[10]
It must not be with this.

CÆS.   You praise yourself
By laying defects of judgement to me, but
You patch'd up your excuses.

ANT.   Not so, not so;
I know you could not lack, I am certain on 't,
Very necessity of this thought, that I,
Your partner in the cause 'gainst which he fought,
Could not with graceful eyes attend those wars
Which fronted mine own peace. As for my wife,
I would you had her spirit in such another:
The third o' the world is yours, which with a snaffle
You may pace easy,[11] but not such a wife.

women as political + martial power!

ENO.   Would we had all such wives, that the men might go to wars
with the women![12]

ANT.   So much uncurbable, her garboils, Cæsar,
Made out of her impatience, which not wanted
Shrewdness of policy too, I grieving grant
Did you too much disquiet: for that you must
But say, I could not help it.

CÆS.   I wrote to you
When rioting in Alexandria; you

---

7. *their contestation . . . for you*] their quarrel had you for its theme.
8. *urge me in his act*] use my name by way of justifying his actions.
9. *patch*] piece together.
10. *As . . . make it with*] since you have no real grounds to base it on.
11. *which with a snaffle . . . pace easy*] which you might govern as easily as you would
guide a horse with a snaffle-bit.
12. *with the women*] with the women on their side.

Did pocket up my letters, and with taunts
Did gibe my missive[13] out of audience.

ANT.   Sir,
He fell upon me ere admitted: then
Three kings I had newly feasted and did want
Of what I was i' the morning:[14] but next day
I told him of myself, which was as much
As to have ask'd him pardon. Let this fellow
Be nothing of our strife; if we contend,
Out of our question wipe him.

CÆS.   You have broken
The article of your oath, which you shall never
Have tongue to charge me with.

LEP.   Soft, Cæsar!

ANT.   No, Lepidus, let him speak:
The honour is sacred which he talks on now,
Supposing that I lack'd it. But on, Cæsar;
The article of my oath.

CÆS.   To lend me arms and aid when I required them;
The which you both denied.

ANT.   Neglected rather,
And then when poison'd hours had bound me up
From mine own knowledge. As nearly as I may,
I'll play the penitent to you: but mine honesty
Shall not make poor my greatness, nor my power
Work without it.[15] Truth is that Fulvia,
To have me out of Egypt, made wars here;
For which myself, the ignorant motive, do
So far ask pardon as befits mine honour
To stoop in such a case.

LEP.   'T is noble spoken.

MÆC.   If it might please you, to enforce no further
The griefs between ye: to forget them quite
Were to remember that the present need
Speaks to atone you.[16]

LEP.   Worthily spoken, Mæcenas.

---

13. *gibe my missive*] ridicule my messenger.
14. *did want . . . the morning*] was not quite myself in the morning.
15. *without it*] without proper regard for my honesty.
16. *atone you*] reconcile you.

ENO. Or, if you borrow one another's love for the instant, you may,
     when you hear no more words of Pompey, return it again: you
     shall have time to wrangle in when you have nothing else to do.

ANT. Thou art a soldier only: speak no more.

ENO. That truth should be silent I had almost forgot.

ANT. You wrong this presence; therefore speak no more.

ENO. Go to, then; your considerate stone.[17]

CÆS. I do not much dislike the matter, but
     The manner of his speech; for 't cannot be
     We shall remain in friendship, our conditions
     So differing in their acts. Yet, if I knew
     What hoop should hold us stanch, from edge to edge
     O' the world I would pursue it.

AGR.   Give me leave, Cæsar.

CÆS. Speak, Agrippa.

AGR. Thou hast a sister by the mother's side,
     Admired Octavia: great Mark Antony
     Is now a widower.

CÆS.   Say not so, Agrippa:
     If Cleopatra heard you, your reproof
     Were well deserved of rashness.

ANT. I am not married, Cæsar: let me hear
     Agrippa further speak.

AGR. ʼTo hold you in perpetual amity,
     To make you brothers and to knit your hearts
     With an unslipping knot, take Antony
     Octavia to his wife; whose beauty claims
     No worse a husband than the best of men,
     Whose virtue and whose general graces speak
     That which none else can utter. By this marriage
     All little jealousies which now seem great,
     And all great fears which now import[18] their dangers,
     Would then be nothing: truths would be tales,
     Where now half tales be truths: her love to both
     Would each to other and all loves to both
     Draw after her. Pardon what I have spoke,
     For 't is a studied, not a present thought,
     By duty ruminated.

---

17. *your considerate stone*] I will be as respectfully silent as a stone.
18. *import*] carry with them.

ANT.   Will Cæsar speak?
CÆS.   Not till he hears how Antony is touch'd
    With what is spoke already.
ANT.   What power is in Agrippa,
    If I would say, "Agrippa, be it so,"
    To make this good?
CÆS.   The power of Cæsar, and
    His power unto Octavia.
ANT.   May I never
    To this good purpose, that so fairly shows,
    Dream of impediment! Let me have thy hand:
    Further this act of grace; and from this hour
    The heart of brothers govern in our loves
    And sway our great designs!
CÆS.   There is my hand.
    A sister I bequeath you, whom no brother
    Did ever love so dearly: let her live
    To join our kingdoms and our hearts; and never
    Fly off our loves again!
LEP.   Happily, amen!
ANT.   I did not think to draw my sword 'gainst Pompey;
    For he hath laid strange courtesies and great
    Of late upon me: I must thank him only,
    Lest my remembrance suffer ill report;
    At heel of that, defy him.
LEP.   Time calls upon 's:
    Of us must Pompey presently be sought,
    Or else he seeks out us.
ANT.   Where lies he?
CÆS.   About the Mount Misenum.[19]
ANT.   What's his strength
    By land?
CÆS.   Great and increasing: but by sea
    He is an absolute master.
ANT.   So is the fame.
    Would we had spoke together! Haste we for it:
    Yet, ere we put ourselves in arms, dispatch we
    The business we have talk'd of.
CÆS.   With most gladness;

---

19. *Misenum*] Punta di Miseno, a promontory of the Bay of Naples.

And do invite you to my sister's view,
Whither straight I'll lead you.
ANT.   Let us, Lepidus,
Not lack your company.
LEP.   Noble Antony,
Not sickness should detain me.
            [*Flourish. Exeunt Cæsar, Antony, and Lepidus.*
MÆC.   Welcome from Egypt, sir.
ENO.   Half the heart of Cæsar, worthy Mæcenas! My honourable
friend, Agrippa!
AGR.   Good Enobarbus!
MÆC.   We have cause to be glad that matters are so well digested. You
stayed well by 't in Egypt.
ENO.   Ay, sir; we did sleep day out of countenance, and made the
night light with drinking.
MÆC.   Eight wild-boars roasted whole at a breakfast, and but twelve
persons there; is this true?
ENO.   This was but as a fly by an eagle: we had much more monstrous
matter of feast, which worthily deserved noting.
MÆC.   She's a most triumphant lady, if report be square to her.[20]
ENO.   When she first met Mark Antony, she pursed up his heart, upon
the river of Cydnus.
AGR.   There she appeared indeed, or my reporter devised well for her.
ENO.   I will tell you.
The barge she sat in, like a burnish'd throne,
Burn'd on the water: the poop was beaten gold;
Purple the sails, and so perfumed that
The winds were love-sick with them; the oars were silver,
Which to the tune of flutes kept stroke and made
The water which they beat to follow faster,
As amorous of their strokes. For her own person,
It beggar'd all description: she did lie
In her pavilion, cloth-of-gold of tissue,[21]
O'er-picturing that Venus where we see
The fancy outwork nature: on each side her
Stood pretty dimpled boys, like smiling Cupids,
With divers-colour'd fans, whose wind did seem

20. *if report be square to her*] if report do her justice.
21. *cloth-of-gold of tissue*] plain cloth embroidered with gold.

Paradoxical

To glow[22] the delicate cheeks which they did cool,
And what they undid did.

AGR.   O, rare for Antony!

ENO.   Her gentlewomen, like the Nereides,[23]
So many mermaids, tended her i' the eyes,[24]
And made their bends adornings: at the helm
A seeming mermaid steers: the silken tackle
Swell with the touches of those flower-soft hands,
That yarely frame the office.[25] From the barge
A strange invisible perfume hits the sense
Of the adjacent wharfs. The city cast
Her people out upon her; and Antony,
Enthroned i' the market-place, did sit alone,
Whistling to the air; which, but for vacancy,[26]
Had gone to gaze on Cleopatra too,
And made a gap in nature.

mythical & trans.   *other worldly*   *awe inspiring*

AGR.   Rare Egyptian!

ENO.   Upon her landing, Antony sent to her,
Invited her to supper: she replied,
It should be better he became her guest,
Which she entreated: our courteous Antony,
Whom ne'er the word of "No" woman heard speak,
Being barber'd ten times o'er, goes to the feast,
And, for his ordinary,[27] pays his heart
For what his eyes eat only.

metaphysical food

AGR.   Royal wench!
She made great Cæsar lay his sword to bed:
He plough'd her, and she cropp'd.

ENO.   I saw her once
Hop forty paces through the public street;
And having lost her breath, she spoke, and panted,
That she did make defect perfection,
And, breathless, power breathe forth.

MÆC.   Now Antony must leave her utterly.

ENO.   Never; he will not: *knows Antony*

22. *glow*] heat, warm.
23. *Nereides*] the sea nymphs attendant upon Neptune.
24. *tended her i' the eyes*] waited on her every look.
25. *yarely frame the office*] deftly perform the tasks they undertake.
26. *but for vacancy*] save that it would have created a vacuum.
27. *ordinary*] properly a dinner at a tavern, for which there is a fixed charge.

Age cannot wither her, nor custom stale
Her infinite variety: other women cloy
The appetites they feed, but she makes hungry
Where most she satisfies: for vilest things
Become themselves in her, that the holy priests
Bless her when she is riggish.[28] (*wanton*)

MÆC.   If beauty, wisdom, modesty, can settle
The heart of Antony, Octavia is
A blessed lottery[29] to him.

AGR.   Let us go.
Good Enobarbus, make yourself my guest
Whilst you abide here.

ENO.   Humbly, sir, I thank you.   [*Exeunt.*

SCENE III. *The Same. Cæsar's House.*

Enter ANTONY, CÆSAR, OCTAVIA *between them, and* Attendants

ANT.   The world and my great office will sometimes
Divide me from your bosom.

OCTA.   All which time
Before the gods my knee shall bow my prayers
To them for you.

ANT.   Good night, sir. My Octavia,
Read not my blemishes in the world's report:
I have not kept my square;[1] but that to come   *admits his failings*
Shall all be done by the rule. Good night, dear lady.
Good night, sir.

CÆS.   Good night.   [*Exeunt all but Antony.*

Enter Soothsayer

ANT.   Now, sirrah, you do wish yourself in Egypt?

28. *riggish*] wanton, immodest.
29. *lottery*] prize.

1. *I have not kept my square*] I have not strictly kept to the path of duty.

SOOTH.   Would I had never come from thence, nor you thither![2]
ANT.   If you can, your reason?
SOOTH.   I see it in my motion,[3] have it not in my tongue: but yet hie
    you to Egypt again.
ANT.   Say to me, whose fortunes shall rise higher, Cæsar's or mine?
SOOTH.   Cæsar's.
    Therefore, O Antony, stay not by his side:
    Thy demon,[4] that thy spirit which keeps thee, is
    Noble, courageous, high, unmatchable,
    Where Cæsar's is not; but near him thy angel
    Becomes a fear, as being o'erpower'd; therefore
    Make space enough between you.
ANT.   Speak this no more.
SOOTH.   To none but thee; no more but when to thee.
    If thou dost play with him at any game,
    Thou art sure to lose; and, of that natural luck,
    He beats thee 'gainst the odds: thy lustre thickens,[5]
    When he shines by: I say again, thy spirit
    Is all afraid to govern thee near him,
    But he away, 'tis noble.
ANT.   Get thee gone:
    Say to Ventidius I would speak with him.   [*Exit Soothsayer.*
    He shall to Parthia. Be it art or hap,
    He hath spoken true: the very dice obey him,
    And in our sports my better cunning faints
    Under his chance: if we draw lots, he speeds;
    His cocks do win the battle still of mine
    When it is all to nought, and his quails ever
    Beat mine, inhoop'd,[6] at odds. I will to Egypt:
    And though I make this marriage for my peace,
    I' the east my pleasure lies.

Enter VENTIDIUS

                              O, come, Ventidius,
    You must to Parthia: your commission's ready;
    Follow me, and receive 't.   [*Exeunt.*

---

2. *nor you thither*] nor you had gone thither.
3. *my motion*] the movement of my mind, my instinct.
4. *demon*] daemon or controlling genius.
5. *thickens*] becomes dark.
6. *inhoop'd*] enclosed in hoops or rings.

SCENE IV. *The Same. A Street.*

Enter LEPIDUS, MÆCENAS, *and* AGRIPPA

LEP.   Trouble yourselves no further: pray you, hasten
     Your generals after.
AGR.   Sir, Mark Antony
     Will e'en but kiss Octavia, and we'll follow.
LEP.   Till I shall see you in your soldier's dress,
     Which will become you both, farewell.
MÆC.   We shall,
     As I conceive the journey, be at the Mount[1]
     Before you, Lepidus.
LEP.   Your way is shorter;
     My purposes do draw me much about:
     You'll win two days upon me.
MÆC. ⎫
AGR. ⎬   Sir, good success!
LEP.   Farewell.   [*Exeunt.*

SCENE V. *Alexandria. Cleopatra's Palace.*

Enter CLEOPATRA, CHARMIAN, IRAS, *and* ALEXAS

CLEO.   Give me some music; music, moody[1] food
     Of us that trade in love.
ALL.   The music, ho!

Enter MARDIAN *the Eunuch*

CLEO.   Let it alone; let's to billiards:[2] come, Charmian.
CHAR.   My arm is sore: best play with Mardian.
CLEO.   As well a woman with an eunuch play'd

   sexual innuendo

---

1. *at the Mount*] Misenum.

---

1. *moody*] melancholy.
2. *billiards*] Cleopatra's reference is anachronistic.

As with a woman. Come, you'll play with me, sir?
MAR.   As well as I can, madam.
CLEO.   And when good will is show'd, though't come too short,
The actor may plead pardon. I'll none now:
Give me mine angle; we'll to the river: there,
My music playing far off, I will betray
Tawny-finn'd fishes; my bended hook shall pierce
Their slimy jaws, and as I draw them up,
I'll think them every one an Antony,
And say "Ah, ha! you're caught."
CHAR.   'Twas merry when
You wager'd on your angling; when your diver
Did hang a salt-fish on his hook, which he
With fervency drew up.
CLEO.   That time—O times!—
I laugh'd him out of patience, and that night
I laugh'd him into patience: and next morn,
Ere the ninth hour, I drunk him to his bed;
Then put my tires[3] and mantles on him, whilst
I wore his sword Philippan.[4]

Enter a Messenger

                              O, from Italy!
Ram thou thy fruitful tidings in mine ears,
That long time have been barren.
MESS.   Madam, madam,—
CLEO.   Antonius dead! If thou say so, villain,
Thou kill'st thy mistress: but well and free,
If thou so yield him, there is gold, and here
My bluest veins to kiss: a hand that kings
Have lipp'd, and trembled kissing.
MESS.   First, madam, he is well.
CLEO.   Why, there's more gold.
But, sirrah, mark, we use
To say the dead are well:[5] bring it to that,
The gold I give thee will I melt and pour
Down thy ill-uttering throat.

---

3. *tires*] head-dresses.
4. *his sword Philippan*] the sword that Antony wore at Philippi.
5. *well*] at rest, happy.

[handwritten at top: Compare her treatment to]

MESS.   Good madam, hear me.
CLEO.   Well, go to, I will;
   But there's no goodness in thy face: if Antony
   Be free and healthful,—so tart a favour[6]
   To trumpet such good tidings! If not well,
   Thou shouldst come like a Fury crown'd with snakes,
   Not like a formal man.[7]
MESS.   Will't please you hear me?
CLEO.   I have a mind to strike thee ere thou speak'st:
   Yet, if thou say Antony lives, is well,
   Or friends with Cæsar, or not captive to him,
   I'll set thee in a shower of gold, and hail
   Rich pearls upon thee.
MESS.   Madam, he's well.
CLEO.   Well said.
MESS.   And friends with Cæsar.
CLEO.   Thou'rt an honest man.
MESS.   Cæsar and he are greater friends than ever.
CLEO.   Make thee a fortune from me.
MESS.   But yet, madam,—
CLEO.   I do not like "But yet," it does allay
   The good precedence;[8] fie upon "But yet"!
   "But yet" is as a gaoler to bring forth
   Some monstrous malefactor. Prithee, friend,
   Pour out the pack of matter to mine ear,
   The good and bad together: he's friends with Cæsar,
   In state of health, thou say'st, and thou say'st, free.
MESS.   Free, madam! no; I made no such report:
   He's bound unto Octavia.
CLEO.   For what good turn?
MESS.   For the best turn i' the bed.   *[handwritten: → unnecessary]*
CLEO.   I am pale, Charmian.   *[handwritten: ⟩ as opposed to colour in her cheek]*
MESS.   Madam, he's married to Octavia.
CLEO.   The most infectious pestilence upon thee! [*Strikes him down.*
MESS.   Good madam, patience.
CLEO.   What say you? Hence,
                 [*Strikes him again.*

---

6. *so tart a favour*] so sour an expression (is not needed).
7. *a formal man*] a man in his senses.
8. *it does allay . . . precedence*] it modifies the pleasurable effect of what precedes.

Horrible villain! or I'll spurn thine eyes
Like balls before me; I'll unhair thy head:

> [*She hales him up and down.*

Thou shalt be whipp'd with wire, and stew'd in brine,
Smarting in lingering pickle.

MESS.   Gracious madam,
I that do bring the news made not the match.

CLEO.   Say 'tis not so, a province I will give thee
And make thy fortunes proud: the blow thou hadst
Shall make thy peace for moving me to rage,
And I will boot thee[9] with what gift beside
Thy modesty can beg.

MESS.   He's married, madam.

CLEO.   Rogue, thou hast lived too long.   [*Draws a knife.*

MESS.   Nay, then, I'll run.
What mean you, madam? I have made no fault.   [*Exit.*

CHAR.   Good madam, keep yourself within yourself:
The man is innocent.

CLEO.   Some innocents 'scape not the thunderbolt.
Melt Egypt into Nile! and kindly creatures
Turn all to serpents! Call the slave again:
Though I am mad, I will not bite him: call.

CHAR.   He is afeard to come.

CLEO.   I will not hurt him.   [*Exit Charmian.*
These hands do lack nobility, that they strike
A meaner than myself; since I myself
Have given myself the cause.[10]

Re-enter CHARMIAN *and* Messenger

                                Come hither, sir.
Though it be honest, it is never good
To bring bad news: give to a gracious message
An host of tongues, but let ill tidings tell
Themselves when they be felt.

MESS.   I have done my duty.

CLEO.   Is he married?
I cannot hate thee worser than I do,

---

9. *boot thee*] endow thee in addition.
10. *since I myself . . . the cause*] Cleopatra possibly means that she gave Antony the opportunity of marriage by suffering him to leave her.

      If thou again say "Yes."

MESS.   He's married, madam.

CLEO.   The gods confound thee! dost thou hold there still?

MESS.   Should I lie, madam?

CLEO.   O, I would thou didst,
      So half my Egypt were submerged and made
      A cistern for scaled snakes! Go get thee hence:
      Hadst thou Narcissus in thy face, to me
      Thou wouldst appear most ugly. He is married?

MESS.   I crave your highness' pardon.

CLEO.   He is married?

MESS.   Take no offence that I would not offend you:[11]
      To punish me for what you make me do
      Seems much unequal: he's married to Octavia.

CLEO.   O, that his fault should make a knave of thee,
      That art not what thou'rt sure of![12] Get thee hence:
      The merchandise which thou hast brought from Rome
      Are all too dear for me: lie they upon thy hand,
      And be undone by 'em!   [Exit Messenger.

CHAR.   Good your highness, patience.

CLEO.   In praising Antony, I have dispraised Cæsar.   *counterpoint*

CHAR.   Many times, madam.

CLEO.   I am paid for 't now.
      Lead me from hence;
      I faint: O Iras, Charmian! 'tis no matter.
      Go to the fellow, good Alexas; bid him
      Report the feature[13] of Octavia, her years,
      Her inclination; let him not leave out
      The colour of her hair: bring me word quickly.   [Exit Alexas.
      Let him for ever go: let him not—Charmian,
      Though he be painted one way like a Gorgon,
      The other way's a Mars.[14] [To Mardian] Bid you Alexas
      Bring me word how tall she is. Pity me, Charmian,
      But do not speak to me. Lead me to my chamber.   [Exeunt.

---

11. *Take no offence . . . offend you*] Do not be offended because I am reluctant to offend you by answering your question again.

12. *That art not . . . of*] that art not the hateful thing of which thou art assured.

13. *feature*] shape, form.

14. *Though he . . . a Mars*] an allusion to a duplicate or convertible picture, which reveals different objects when regarded from different perspectives.

SCENE VI. *Near Misenum.*

Flourish, Enter POMPEY *and* MENAS *from one side, with drum and trumpet: at another,* CÆSAR, ANTONY, LEPIDUS, ENOBARBUS, MÆCENAS, *with* Soldiers *marching*

POM.   Your hostages I have, so have you mine;
  And we shall talk before we fight.
CÆS.   Most meet
  That first we come to words; and therefore have we
  Our written purposes before us sent;
  Which, if thou hast consider'd, let us know
  If 't will tie up thy discontented sword
  And carry back to Sicily much tall youth
  That else must perish here.
POM.   To you all three,
  The senators alone of this great world,
  Chief factors[1] for the gods, I do not know
  Wherefore my father should revengers want,
  Having a son and friends; since Julius Cæsar,
  Who at Philippi the good Brutus ghosted,[2]
  There saw you labouring for him. What was 't
  That moved pale Cassius to conspire, and what
  Made the all-honour'd honest Roman, Brutus,
  With the arm'd rest, courtiers of beauteous freedom,
  To drench the Capitol, but that they would
  Have one man but a man? And that is it
  Hath made me rig my navy, at whose burthen
  The anger'd ocean foams; with which I meant
  To scourge the ingratitude that despiteful Rome
  Cast on my noble father.
CÆS.   Take your time.
ANT.   Thou canst not fear[3] us, Pompey, with thy sails;
  We 'll speak with thee at sea: at land, thou know'st
  How much we do o'ercount thee.
POM.   At land indeed

---

1. *factors*] agents.
2. *ghosted*] haunted.
3. *fear*] frighten.

Thou dost o'ercount me of my father's house:[4]
But since the cuckoo builds not for himself,
Remain in 't as thou mayst.
LEP.   Be pleased to tell us—
For this is from the present[5]—how you take
The offers we have sent you.
CÆS.   There's the point.
ANT.   Which do not be entreated to, but weigh
What it is worth embraced.[6]
CÆS.   And what may follow,
To try a larger fortune.[7]
POM.   You have made me offer
Of Sicily, Sardinia; and I must
Rid all the sea of pirates; then, to send
Measures of wheat to Rome; this 'greed upon,
To part with unhack'd edges and bear back
Our targes[8] undinted.
CÆS.
ANT.   That's our offer.
LEP.
POM.   Know then,
I came before you here a man prepared
To take this offer: but Mark Antony
Put me to some impatience: though I lose
The praise of it by telling, you must know,
When Cæsar and your brother were at blows,
Your mother came to Sicily and did find
Her welcome friendly.
ANT.   I have heard it, Pompey,
And am well studied for a liberal thanks[9]
Which I do owe you.
POM.   Let me have your hand:
I did not think, sir, to have met you here.
ANT.   The beds i' the east are soft; and thanks to you,

---

4. *Thou dost . . . house*] Antony had purchased at auction the mansion of Pompey the
   Great, father of the speaker.
5. *from the present*] foreign to the subject at hand.
6. *embraced*] if accepted.
7. *To try a larger fortune*] if you seek to win more from fortune.
8. *targes*] shields.
9. *studied for a liberal thanks*] prepared to give you a full measure of thanks.

That call'd me timelier than my purpose hither;
For I have gain'd by 't.

CÆS.   Since I saw you last,
There is a change upon you.

POM.   Well, I know not
What counts[10] harsh fortune casts upon my face;
But in my bosom shall she never come,
To make my heart her vassal.

LEP.   Well met here.

POM.   I hope so, Lepidus. Thus we are agreed:
I crave our composition may be written
And seal'd between us.

CÆS.   That's the next to do.

POM.   We'll feast each other ere we part, and let's
Draw lots who shall begin.

ANT.   That will I, Pompey.

POM.   No, Antony, take the lot:
But, first or last, your fine Egyptian cookery
Shall have the fame. I have heard that Julius Cæsar
Grew fat with feasting there.

ANT.   You have heard much.

POM.   I have fair meanings, sir.

ANT.   And fair words to them.

POM.   Then so much have I heard:
And I have heard, Apollodorus carried—

ENO.   No more of that: he did so.

POM.   What, I pray you?

ENO.   A certain queen to Cæsar in a mattress.[11]

POM.   I know thee now: how farest thou, soldier?

ENO.   Well;
And well am like to do, for I perceive
Four feasts are toward.

POM.   Let me shake thy hand;
I never hated thee: I have seen thee fight,
When I have envied thy behaviour.

ENO.   Sir,

---

10. *counts*] marks, lines.
11. *Apollodorus . . . mattress*] According to Plutarch, Cleopatra, having been driven
    from Alexandria by Cæsar, induced Apollodorus to carry her back to the city
    wrapped in a mattress, and to deposit her secretly in Cæsar's quarters.

Sea battle

I never loved you much, but I ha' praised ye
When you have well deserved ten times as much
As I have said you did.

POM.   Enjoy thy plainness,
It nothing ill becomes thee.
Aboard my galley I invite you all:
Will you lead, lords?

CÆS. ⎤
ANT. ⎬   Show us the way, sir.
LEP. ⎦

POM.   Come.

[*Exeunt all but Menas and Enobarbus.*

MEN.   [*Aside*] Thy father, Pompey, would ne'er have made this
   treaty.—You and I have known, sir.   — *gave in too easily*
ENO.   At sea, I think.
MEN.   We have, sir.
ENO.   You have done well by water.
MEN.   And you by land.
ENO.   I will praise any man that will praise me; though it cannot be
   denied what I have done by land.
MEN.   Nor what I have done by water.
ENO.   Yes, something you can deny for your own safety: you have
   been a great thief by sea.
MEN.   And you by land.
ENO.   There I deny my land service. But give me your hand, Menas:
   if our eyes had authority, here they might take two thieves kissing.
MEN.   All men's faces are true, whatsoe'er their hands are.
ENO.   But there is never a fair woman has a true face.
MEN.   No slander; they steal hearts.
ENO.   We came hither to fight with you.
MEN.   For my part, I am sorry it is turned to a drinking. Pompey doth
   this day laugh away his fortune.   *Antony laves away his*
ENO.   If he do, sure he cannot weep 't back again.
MEN.   You've said, sir. We looked not for Mark Antony here: pray you,
   is he married to Cleopatra?
ENO.   Cæsar's sister is called Octavia.
MEN.   True, sir; she was the wife of Caius Marcellus.
ENO.   But she is now the wife of Marcus Antonius.
MEN.   Pray ye, sir?
ENO.   'T is true.
MEN.   Then is Cæsar and he for ever knit together.

language of state not love.

ENO.   If I were bound to divine of this unity, I would not prophesy so.

MEN.   I think the policy of that purpose made more in the marriage than the love of the parties.

ENO.   I think so too. But you shall find, the band that seems to tie their friendship together will be the very strangler of their amity: Octavia is of a holy, cold and still conversation. — *very opposite to*

MEN.   Who would not have his wife so?

ENO.   Not he that himself is not so; which is Mark Antony. He will to his Egyptian dish again: then shall the sighs of Octavia blow the fire up in Cæsar; and, as I said before, that which is the strength of their amity shall prove the immediate author of their variance. Antony will use his affection where it is: he married but his occasion[12] here.

MEN.   And thus it may be. Come, sir, will you aboard? I have a health for you.

ENO.   I shall take it, sir: we have used our throats in Egypt.

MEN.   Come, let's away.   [*Exeunt.*

SCENE VII. *On Board Pompey's Galley, off Misenum.*

Music plays. Enter two or three Servants, *with a banquet*[1]

FIRST SERV.   Here they'll be, man. Some o' their plants[2] are ill-rooted already; the least wind i' the world will blow them down.   *drunk*

SEC. SERV.   Lepidus is high-coloured. — *red*

FIRST SERV.   They have made him drink alms-drink.[3]

SEC. SERV.   As they pinch one another by the disposition,[4] he cries out "No more;" reconciles them to his entreaty and himself to the drink.

---

12. *occasion*] convenience.

---

1. *a banquet*] the dessert following the great meal.
2. *plants*] humorously used for the soles of the feet, like the Latin "plantae."
3. *alms-drink*] dregs. Apparently Lepidus has been induced to drink the leavings in his host's glasses in the drunken way of good fellowship.
4. *pinch . . . disposition*] chafe one another, challenging each other's prowess at drinking.

FIRST SERV.   But it raises the greater war between him and his discre-
tion.

SEC. SERV.   Why, this it is to have a name in great men's fellowship: I
had as lief have a reed that will do me no service as a partisan[5] I
could not heave.

FIRST. SERV.   To be called into a huge sphere, and not to be seen to
move in 't, are the holes where eyes should be, which pitifully disaster[6] the cheeks.

A sennet sounded. Enter CÆSAR, ANTONY, LEPIDUS, POMPEY, AGRIPPA,
MÆCENAS, ENOBARBUS, MENAS, *with other captains*

ANT.   [*To Cæsar*] Thus do they, sir: they take the flow o' the Nile
By certain scales i' the pyramid; they know,
By the height, the lowness, or the mean, if dearth
Or foison[7] follow: the higher Nilus swells,
The more it promises: as it ebbs, the seedsman
Upon the slime and ooze scatters his grain,
And shortly comes to harvest.

LEP.   You've strange serpents there.

ANT.   Ay, Lepidus.

LEP.   Your serpent of Egypt is bred now of your mud by the operation
of your sun: so is your crocodile.

ANT.   They are so.

POM.   Sit,—and some wine! A health to Lepidus!

LEP.   I am not so well as I should be, but I'll ne'er out.[8]

ENO.   Not till you have slept; I fear me you'll be in[9] till then.

LEP.   Nay, certainly, I have heard the Ptolemies' pyramises are very
goodly things; without contradiction, I have heard that.

MEN.   [*Aside to Pom.*] Pompey, a word.

POM.   [*Aside to Men.*] Say in mine ear: what is 't?

MEN.   [*Aside to Pom.*] Forsake thy seat, I do beseech thee, captain,
And hear me speak a word.

POM.   [*Aside to Men.*] Forbear me till anon.—
This wine for Lepidus!

LEP.   What manner o' thing is your crocodile?

---

5. *partisan*] halberd.
6. *disaster*] disfigure.
7. *foison*] abundance.
8. *I'll ne'er out*] I will not leave the party.
9. *you'll be in*] you'll be under the influence of drink.

ANT.   It is shaped, sir, like itself; and it is as broad as it hath breadth:
   it is just so high as it is, and moves with it own organs:[10] it lives by
   that which nourisheth it; and the elements once out of it, it trans-
   migrates.

LEP.   What colour is it of?

ANT.   Of it own colour too.

LEP.   'T is a strange serpent.

ANT.   'T is so. And the tears of it are wet.

CÆS.   Will this description satisfy him?

ANT.   With the health that Pompey gives him, else he is a very
   epicure.

POM.   [*Aside to Men.*] Go hang, sir, hang! Tell me of that? away!
   Do as I bid you. —Where 's this cup I call'd for?

MEN.   [*Aside to Pom.*] If for the sake of merit thou wilt hear me,
   Rise from thy stool.

POM.   [*Aside to Men.*] I think thou 'rt mad. The matter?
                                                     [*Rises, and walks aside.*

MEN.   I have ever held my cap off to thy fortunes.

POM.   Thou hast served me with much faith. What 's else to say?
   Be jolly, lords.

ANT.   These quick-sands, Lepidus,
   Keep off them, for you sink.

MEN.   Wilt thou be lord of all the world?

POM.   What say'st thou?

MEN.   Wilt thou be lord of the whole world? That 's twice.

POM.   How should that be?

MEN.   But entertain it,
   And, though thou think me poor, I am the man
   Will give thee all the world.

POM.   Hast thou drunk well?

MEN.   No, Pompey, I have kept me from the cup.
   Thou art, if thou darest be, the earthly Jove:
   Whate'er the ocean pales, or sky inclips,[11]
   Is thine, if thou wilt ha 't.

POM.   Show me which way.

MEN.   These three world-sharers, these competitors,
   Are in thy vessel: let me cut the cable;
   And, when we are put off, fall to their throats:

---

10. *it own organs*] "it" is the old form of "its."
11. *Whate'er . . . inclips*] whatever the ocean surrounds or the sky embraces.

the situation of politics

          All there is thine.
POM.   Ah, this thou shouldst have done,
     And not have spoke on 't! In me 'tis villany;
     In thee 't had been good service. Thou must know,
     'T is not my profit that does lead mine honour;
     Mine honour, it.[12] Repent that e'er thy tongue
     Hath so betray'd thine act: being done unknown,
     I should have found it afterwards well done,
     But must condemn it now. Desist, and drink.
MEN.   [*Aside*] For this
     I 'll never follow thy pall'd fortunes more.
     Who seeks, and will not take when once 'tis offer'd,
     Shall never find it more.
POM.   This health to Lepidus!
ANT.   Bear him ashore. I 'll pledge it for him, Pompey.
ENO.   Here 's to thee, Menas!
MEN.   Enobarbus, welcome!
POM.   Fill till the cup be hid.
ENO.   There 's a strong fellow, Menas.
                    [*Pointing to the Attendant who carries off Lepidus.*
MEN.   Why?
ENO.   A' bears the third part of the world, man; see 'st not?
MEN.   The third part then is drunk: would it were all,
     That it might go on wheels![13]
ENO.   Drink thou; increase the reels.
MEN.   Come.
POM.   This is not yet an Alexandrian feast.
ANT.   It ripens towards it. Strike the vessels,[14] ho!
     Here 's to Cæsar!
CÆS.   I could well forbear 't.
     It 's monstrous labour, when I wash my brain
     And it grows fouler.
ANT.   Be a child o' the time.[15]
CÆS.   Possess it,[16] I 'll make answer:
     But I had rather fast from all four days

---

12. *Mine honour, it*] My profit is not a primary consideration.
13. *go on wheels*] whirl round, change its course.
14. *Strike the vessels*] Broach the casks.
15. *Be a child o' the time*] Comply with the humor of the minute.
16. *Possess it*] have it your way.

Than drink so much in one.

ENO.   *[To Antony]* Ha, my brave emperor!
 Shall we dance now the Egyptian Bacchanals,
 And celebrate our drink?

POM.   Let's ha't, good soldier.

ANT. Come, let's all take hands,
 Till that the conquering wine hath steep'd our sense
 In soft and delicate Lethe.

ENO.   All take hands.
 Make battery to our ears with the loud music:
 The while I'll place you: then the boy shall sing;
 The holding[17] every man shall bear as loud
 As his strong sides can volley.

     [Music plays. Enobarbus places them hand in hand.

THE SONG.

   Come, thou monarch of the vine,
   Plumpy Bacchus with pink eyne![18]
   In thy fats[19] our cares be drown'd,
   With thy grapes our hairs be crown'd:
   Cup us, till the world go round,
   Cup us, till the world go round!

CÆS. What would you more? Pompey, good night. Good brother,
 Let me request you off: our graver business
 Frowns at this levity. Gentle lords, let's part;
 You see we have burnt our cheeks: strong Enobarb
 Is weaker than the wine; and mine own tongue
 Splits what it speaks: the wild disguise[20] hath almost
 Antick'd[21] us all. What needs more words? Good night.
 Good Antony, your hand.

POM.   I'll try you on the shore.

ANT. And shall, sir: give's your hand.

POM.   O Antony,
 You have my father's house,—But, what? we are friends.

---

17. *holding*] burden or chorus.
18. *pink eyne*] half-shut eyes.
19. *fats*] vats, vessels.
20. *disguise*] drunkenness.
21. *Antick'd*] made into buffoons.

Come, down into the boat.

ENO.   Take heed you fall not.

[*Exeunt all but Enobarbus and Menas.*

Menas, I'll not on shore.

MEN.   No, to my cabin.

These drums! these trumpets, flutes! what!
Let Neptune hear we bid a loud farewell
To these great fellows: sound and be hang'd, sound out!

[*Sound a flourish, with drums.*

ENO.   Hoo! says a'. There's my cap.

MEN.   Hoo! Noble captain, come.   [*Exeunt.*

[handwritten: Opens the play up — reveals the scope of the world / staging of the play]

ACT III.

SCENE I. A *Plain in Syria.*

[handwritten: underlings win wars]

Enter VENTIDIUS *as it were in triumph, with* SILIUS, *and other* Romans, Officers, *and* Soldiers; *the dead body of* PACORUS *borne before him*

VENTIDIUS.   Now, darting Parthia,[1] art thou struck; and now
    Pleased fortune does of Marcus Crassus' death
    Make me revenger. Bear the king's son's body
    Before our army. Thy Pacorus, Orodes,
    Pays this for Marcus Crassus.[2]

[handwritten: Historical context]

SIL.   Noble Ventidius,
    Whilst yet with Parthian blood thy sword is warm,
    The fugitive Parthians follow; spur through Media,
    Mesopotamia, and the shelters whither
    The routed fly: so thy grand captain Antony
    Shall set thee on triumphant chariots and
    Put garlands on thy head.

[handwritten: celebrate your success]

VEN.   O Silius, Silius,
    I have done enough: a lower place, note well,
    May make too great an act;[3] for learn this, Silius,
    Better to leave undone than by our deed
    Acquire too high a fame when him we serve 's away.
    Cæsar and Antony have ever won
    More in their officer than person: Sossius,
    One of my place in Syria, his lieutenant,
    For quick accumulation of renown,
    Which he achieved by the minute, lost his favour.
    Who does i' the wars more than his captain can

1. *darting Parthia*] Parthia's mounted archers were renowned for their skill.
2. *Marcus Crassus*] Ventidius' decisive defeat of the Parthians and slaughter of their king Pacorus took place in 39 B.C., fourteen years after King Pacorus' father Orodes had destroyed the Roman general Marcus Crassus and a great Roman army.
3. *a lower place . . . an act*] one of lower rank may win more glory than becomes his station.

46

wins wars & empires

Becomes his captain's captain: and ambition,
The soldier's virtue, rather makes choice of loss
Than gain which darkens him.[4]
I could do more to do Antonius good,
But 't would offend him, and in his offence   *pun on word*
Should my performance perish.

SIL.   Thou hast, Ventidius, that
Without the which a soldier and his sword
Grants scarce distinction. Thou wilt write to Antony?

VEN.   I'll humbly signify what in his name,
That magical word of war, we have effected;
How, with his banners and his well-paid ranks,
The ne'er-yet-beaten horse of Parthia
We have jaded out o' the field.

SIL.   Where is he now?

VEN.   He purposeth to Athens: whither, with what haste
The weight we must convey with 's will permit,
We shall appear before him. On, there; pass along!   [*Exeunt.*

SCENE II. *Rome. An Ante-Chamber in Cæsar's House.*

Stage directions

Enter AGRIPPA *at one door, and* ENOBARBUS *at another*

AGR.   What, are the brothers parted?

ENO.   They have dispatch'd[1] with Pompey; he is gone;
The other three are sealing.[2] Octavia weeps
To part from Rome; Cæsar is sad, and Lepidus
Since Pompey's feast, as Menas says, is troubled
With the green sickness.[3] *ridiculing*

AGR.   'T is a noble Lepidus.

ENO.   A very fine one: O, how he loves Cæsar!

---

4. *gain which darkens him*] gain which puts the captain in the shade.

1. *dispatch'd*] settled matters.
2. *sealing*] signing the agreements.
3. *the green sickness*] an anemic complaint from which young girls in love often suffer;
   Enobarbus is perhaps ridiculing Lepidus' affection for Cæsar and Antony.

AGR.   Nay, but how dearly he adores Mark Antony!
ENO.   Cæsar? Why, he's the Jupiter of men.
AGR.   What's Antony? The god of Jupiter.
ENO.   Spake you of Cæsar? How! the nonpareil![4]
AGR.   O Antony! O thou Arabian bird![5]
ENO.   Would you praise Cæsar, say "Cæsar": go no further.
AGR.   Indeed, he plied them both with excellent praises.
ENO.   But he loves Cæsar best; yet he loves Antony:
  Ho! hearts, tongues, figures, scribes, bards, poets, cannot
  Think, speak, cast, write, sing, number—ho!—
  His love to Antony. But as for Cæsar,
  Kneel down, kneel down, and wonder.
AGR.   Both he loves.
ENO.   They are his shards,[6] and he their beetle. [*Trumpet within.*] So;
  This is to horse. Adieu, noble Agrippa.
AGR.   Good fortune, worthy soldier, and farewell.

Enter CÆSAR, ANTONY, LEPIDUS, *and* OCTAVIA

ANT.   No further, sir.
CÆS.   You take from me a great part of myself;
  Use me well in 't. Sister, prove such a wife
  As my thoughts make thee, and as my farthest band
  Shall pass on thy approof.[7] Most noble Antony,
  Let not the piece[8] of virtue which is set
  Betwixt us as the cement of our love,
  To keep it builded, be the ram to batter
  The fortress of it; for better might we
  Have loved without this mean, if on both parts
  This be not cherish'd.
ANT.   Make me not offended
  In your distrust.
CÆS.   I have said.
ANT.   You shall not find,
  Though you be therein curious,[9] the least cause

[margin handwritten note:] —willing to use her.

---

4. *nonpareil*] paragon.
5. *Arabian bird*] the phoenix.
6. *shards*] the wing cases of beetles.
7. *as my farthest band . . . approof*] such that my strongest pledge shall be confirmed by the trial of thy conduct.
8. *piece*] masterpiece.
9. *curious*] over-cautious.

For what you seem to fear: so, the gods keep you,
And make the hearts of Romans serve your ends!
We will here part.

CÆS. Farewell, my dearest sister, fare thee well:
The elements be kind to thee, and make
Thy spirits all of comfort! fare thee well.

OCTA. My noble brother!

ANT. The April's in her eyes: it is love's spring,
And these the showers to bring it on. Be cheerful.

Octavia says little.

OCTA. Sir, look well to my husband's house, and—

CÆS.   What,
Octavia?

OCTA. I'll tell you in your ear.

ANT. Her tongue will not obey her heart, nor can
Her heart inform her tongue, the swan's down-feather,
That stands upon the swell at full of tide
And neither way inclines.[10]

→ imagery

ENO. [Aside to Agr.] Will Cæsar weep?

AGR.   [Aside to Eno.] He has a cloud in 's face.

ENO. [Aside to Agr.] He were the worse for that, were he a horse;[11]
So is he, being a man.

AGR. [Aside to Eno.] Why, Enobarbus,
When Antony found Julius Cæsar dead,
He cried almost to roaring; and he wept
When at Philippi he found Brutus slain.

ENO. [Aside to Agr.] That year indeed he was troubled with a rheum;[12]
What willingly he did confound[13] he wail'd,
Believe 't, till I wept too.

CÆS.   No, sweet Octavia,
You shall hear from me still; the time shall not
Out-go my thinking on you.

ANT.   Come, sir, come;
I'll wrestle with you in my strength of love:
Look, here I have you; thus I let you go,
And give you to the gods.

10. *Her tongue . . . inclines*] Octavia's affections are equally divided between her
    brother and her husband.
11. *were he a horse*] a horse with no white on its forehead was said to have "a cloud in
    the face," i.e., to be of sullen disposition.
12. *a rheum*] a cold in the head, which made his eyes water.
13. *confound*] destroy or ruin.

CÆS. Adieu; be happy!
LEP. Let all the number of the stars give light
   To thy fair way!
CÆS. Farewell, farewell! [*Kisses Octavia.*
ANT. Farewell!
                         [*Trumpets sound. Exeunt.*

SCENE III. *Alexandria. Cleopatra's Palace.*

Enter CLEOPATRA, CHARMIAN, IRAS, *and* ALEXAS

CLEO. Where is the fellow?
ALEX. Half afeard to come. — *because of*
CLEO. Go to, go to. *her actions in!*

Enter Messenger

                 Come hither, sir.
ALEX. Good majesty.
   Herod of Jewry dare not look upon you
   But when you are well pleased.
CLEO. That Herod's head
   I'll have: but how, when Antony is gone
   Through whom I might command it? Come thou near.
MESS. Most gracious majesty,—
CLEO. Didst thou behold
   Octavia?
MESS. Ay, dread queen.
CLEO. Where?
MESS. Madam, in Rome
   I look'd her in the face, and saw her led
   Between her brother and Mark Antony.
CLEO. Is she as tall as me?
MESS. She is not, madam.
CLEO. Didst hear her speak? is she shrill-tongued or low?
MESS. Madam, I heard her speak; she is low-voiced.
CLEO. That 's not so good. He cannot like her long.
CHAR. Like her! O Isis! 'tis impossible.

CLEO.   I think so, Charmian: dull of tongue and dwarfish.
        What majesty is in her gait? Remember,
        If e'er thou look'dst on majesty.
MESS.   She creeps:
        Her motion and her station[1] are as one;
        She shows a body rather than a life,
        A statue than a breather.[2]

Hearing what she wants for

CLEO.   Is this certain?
MESS.   Or I have no observance.
CHAR.   Three in Egypt
        Cannot make better note.
CLEO.   He's very knowing;
        I do perceive 't: there's nothing in her yet:
        The fellow has good judgement.
CHAR.   Excellent.
CLEO.   Guess at her years, I prithee.
MESS.   Madam,
        She was a widow—
CLEO.   Widow! Charmian, hark.
MESS.   And I do think she's thirty.
CLEO.   Bear'st thou her face in mind? is 't long or round?
MESS.   Round even to faultiness.
CLEO.   For the most part, too, they are foolish that are so.
        Her hair, what colour?
MESS.   Brown, madam: and her forehead
        As low as she would wish it.[3]
CLEO.   There's gold for thee.
        Thou must not take my former sharpness ill:
        I will employ thee back again; I find thee
        Most fit for business: go make thee ready;
        Our letters are prepared.   [*Exit Messenger.*
CHAR.   A proper man.
CLEO.   Indeed, he is so: I repent me much
        That so I harried him. Why, methinks, by him,
        This creature's no such thing.
CHAR.   Nothing, madam.

1. *station*] standing.
2. *a breather*] a living person.
3. *As low as she would wish it*] so low that she could not wish it lower. A low forehead
   was reckoned a deformity.

CLEO.　The man hath seen some majesty, and should know.
CHAR.　Hath he seen majesty? Isis else defend,[4]
　　And serving you so long!
CLEO.　I have one thing more to ask him yet, good Charmian:
　　But 'tis no matter; thou shalt bring him to me
　　Where I will write. All may be well enough.
CHAR.　I warrant you, madam.　　　　　　　　　[*Exeunt.*

SCENE IV. *Athens. A Room in Antony's House.*

Enter ANTONY *and* OCTAVIA

Caesar attacks P after treaty

ANT.　Nay, nay, Octavia, not only that,
　　That were excusable, that and thousands more
　　Of semblable[1] import, but he hath waged
　　New wars 'gainst Pompey; made his will, and read it
　　To public ear:
disrespected Spoke scantly[2] of me: when perforce he could not
　　But pay me terms of honour, cold and sickly
　　He vented them; most narrow measure lent me;
　　When the best hint was given him, he not took 't,
　　Or did it from his teeth.[3]
OCTA.　　　　　　　　　　O my good lord,
　　Believe not all; or, if you must believe,
　　Stomach[4] not all. A more unhappy lady,
　　If this division chance, ne'er stood between,
← 　Praying for both parts:
her position is untenable,
　　The good gods will mock me presently,
　　When I shall pray, "O, bless my lord and husband!"
　　Undo that prayer, by crying out as loud,
　　"O, bless my brother!" Husband win, win brother,

4. *Isis else defend*] God forbid.

counterpoint

1. *semblable*] similar.
2. *scantly*] grudgingly.
3. *from his teeth*] insincerely, with the merest formality.
4. *Stomach*] resent, show anger at.

     Prays, and destroys the prayer; no midway
     'Twixt these extremes at all.

ANT.   Gentle Octavia,
     Let your best love draw to that point, which seeks
     Best to preserve it; if I lose mine honour,
     I lose myself: better I were not yours
     Than yours so branchless. But, as you requested,
     Yourself shall go between 's: the mean time, lady,
     I'll raise the preparation of a war
     Shall stain[5] your brother: make your soonest haste;
     So your desires are yours.

OCTA.   Thanks to my lord.
     The Jove of power make me most weak, most weak,
     Your reconciler! Wars 'twixt you twain would be
     As if the world should cleave, and that slain men
     Should solder up the rift.

ANT.   When it appears to you where this begins,
     Turn your displeasure that way; for our faults
     Can never be so equal, that your love
     Can equally move with them. Provide your going;
     Choose your own company, and command what cost
     Your heart has mind to.   [*Exeunt.*

SCENE V. *The Same. Another Room.*

Enter ENOBARBUS *and* EROS, *meeting*

ENO.   How now, friend Eros!

EROS.   There 's strange news come, sir.

ENO.   What, man?

EROS.   Cæsar and Lepidus have made wars upon Pompey.

ENO.   This is old: what is the success?[1]

EROS.   Cæsar, having made use of him in the wars 'gainst Pompey,

---

5. *stain*] eclipse.

---

1. *success*] result, consequence.

Death of Lepidus

presently denied him rivality;[2] would not let him partake in the
glory of the action: and not resting here, accuses him of letters he
had formerly wrote to Pompey; upon his own appeal, seizes him:
so the poor third is up,[3] till death enlarge his confine.

ENO.   Then, world, thou hast a pair of chaps,[4] no more;
   And throw between them all the food thou hast,   *} food
   They'll grind the one the other. Where's Antony?   Imagery*

EROS.   He's walking in the garden—thus; and spurns
   The rush that lies before him; cries "Fool Lepidus!"
   And threats the throat of that his officer
   That murder'd Pompey.

ENO.   Our great navy's rigg'd.

EROS.   For Italy and Cæsar. More, Domitius;
   My lord desires you presently: my news
   I might have told hereafter.

ENO.   'T will be naught:
   But let it be. Bring me to Antony.

EROS.   Come, sir.   [*Exeunt.*

SCENE VI. *Rome. Cæsar's House.*

Enter CÆSAR, AGRIPPA, *and* MÆCENAS

CÆS.   Contemning Rome, he has done all this, and more,
   In Alexandria: here's the manner of 't:
   I' the market-place, on a tribunal silver'd
   Cleopatra and himself in chairs of gold
   Were publicly enthroned: at the feet sat
   Cæsarion, whom they call my father's son,[1]
   And all the unlawful issue that their lust
   Since then hath made between them. Unto her

---

2. *rivality*] partnership, equality of power.
3. *is up*] is done with.
4. *chaps*] jaws.

---

1. *my father's son*] Julius Cæsar, who was father of Cæsarian by Cleopatra, had adopted
   Octavius Cæsar his grand-nephew as his son.

Terrority = power = ownership

He gave the stablishment of Egypt; made her
Of lower Syria, Cyprus, Lydia,
<u>Absolute queen.</u>
MÆC.   This in the public eye?
CÆS.   I' the common show-place, where they exercise.
His sons he there proclaim'd the kings of kings:
Great Media, Parthia and Armenia
He gave to Alexander; to Ptolemy he assign'd
Syria, Cilicia and Phœnicia: she
In the habiliments of the <u>goddess Isis</u>   ✗
That day appear'd, and oft before gave audience,
As 't is reported, so.
MÆC.   Let Rome be thus
Inform'd.
AGR.   Who, queasy with his insolence
Already, will their good thoughts call from him.
CÆS.   The people know it, and have now received
His accusations.
AGR.   Who does he accuse?
CÆS.   Cæsar: and that, having in Sicily
Sextus Pompeius spoil'd, we had not rated² him
His part o' the isle: then does he say, he lent me
Some shipping unrestored: lastly, he frets
That Lepidus of the triumvirate
Should be deposed; and, being,³ that we detain
All his revenue.
AGR.   Sir, this should be answer'd.
CÆS.   'T is done already, and the messenger gone.
I have told him, <u>Lepidus was grown too cruel;</u>   — _ridiculous!_
That he his high authority abused
And did deserve his change: for what I have conquer'd,
I grant him part; but then, in his Armenia
And other of his conquer'd kingdoms, I
Demand the like.
MÆC.   He 'll never yield to that.   _untenable_
CÆS.   Nor must not then be yielded to in this.   _situation._

Enter OCTAVIA, _with her train_

2. _rated_] allotted.
3. _being_] that being so.

OCTA.   Hail, Cæsar, and my lord! hail, most dear Cæsar!
CÆS.   That ever I should call thee castaway!
OCTA.   You have not call'd me so, nor have you cause.
CÆS.   Why have you stol'n upon us thus? You come not
    Like Cæsar's sister: the wife of Antony
    Should have an army for an usher, and
    The neighs of horse to tell of her approach
    Long ere she did appear; the trees by the way
    Should have borne men; and expectation fainted,
    Longing for what it had not; nay, the dust
    Should have ascended to the roof of heaven,
    Raised by your populous troops: but you are come
    A market-maid to Rome; and have prevented
    The ostentation[4] of our love, which, left unshown,
    Is often left unloved:[5] we should have met you
    By sea and land, supplying every stage
    With an augmented greeting.
OCTA.   Good my lord,
    To come thus was I not constrain'd, but did it
    On my free will. My lord, Mark Antony,
    Hearing that you prepared for war, acquainted
    My grieved ear withal; whereon, I begg'd
    His pardon for return.
CÆS.   Which soon he granted,
    Being an obstruct 'tween his lust and him.
OCTA.   Do not say so, my lord.
CÆS.   I have eyes[6] upon him,
    And his affairs come to me on the wind.
    Where is he now?
OCTA.   My lord, in Athens.
CÆS.   No, my most wronged sister; Cleopatra
    Hath nodded him to her. He hath given his empire
    Up to a whore; who now are levying
    The kings o' the earth for war: he hath assembled
    Bocchus, the king of Libya; Archelaus,
    Of Cappadocia; Philadelphos, king

[handwritten marginal note: No Pomp ↓ trapping of office power]

4. *ostentation*] manifestation.
5. *unloved*] unvalued.
6. *eyes*] spies.

    Of Paphlagonia; the Thracian king, Adallas;
    King Malchus of Arabia; King of Pont;
    Herod of Jewry; Mithridates, king
    Of Comagene; Polemon and Amyntas,
    The kings of Mede and Lycaonia,
    With a more larger list of sceptres.
OCTA.   Ay me, most wretched,
    That have my heart parted betwixt two friends
    That do afflict each other!
CÆS.   Welcome hither:
    Your letters did withhold our breaking forth,
    Till we perceived both how you were wrong led
    And we in negligent danger.[7] Cheer your heart:
    Be you not troubled with the time, which drives
    O'er your content these strong necessities;
    But let determined things to destiny[8]
    Hold unbewail'd their way. Welcome to Rome;
    Nothing more dear to me. You are abused
    Beyond the mark of thought: and the high gods,
    To do you justice, make them ministers
    Of us and those that love you. Best of comfort;
    And ever welcome to us.
AGR.   Welcome, lady.
MÆC.   Welcome, dear madam.
    Each heart in Rome does love and pity you:
    Only the adulterous Antony, most large
    In his abominations, turns you off;
    And gives his potent regiment to a trull,
    That noises it against us.[9]
OCTA.   Is it so, sir?
CÆS.   Most certain. Sister, welcome: pray you,
    Be ever known to patience: my dear'st sister!   [*Exeunt.*

---

7. *negligent danger*] danger from negligence.
8. *determined things to destiny*] things already fixed by destiny.
9. *gives . . . against us*] gives his powerful authority to a harlot, that raises loud voice of
   opposition against us.

SCENE VII. *Near Actium. Antony's Camp.*

Enter CLEOPATRA *and* ENOBARBUS

CLEO.   I will be even with thee, doubt it not.
ENO.   But why, why, why?
CLEO.   Thou hast forspoke[1] my being in these wars,
    And say'st it is not fit.
ENO.   Well, is it, is it?
CLEO.   If not denounced against us, why should not we
    Be there in person?
ENO.   [*Aside*] Well, I could reply:
    If we should serve with horse and mares together,
    The horse were merely[2] lost; the mares would bear
    A soldier and his horse.
CLEO.   What is 't you say?
ENO.   Your presence needs must puzzle[3] Antony;
    Take from his heart, take from his brain, from 's time,
    What should not then be spared. He is already
    Traduced for levity; and 't is said in Rome
    That Photinus, an eunuch and your maids
    Manage this war.
CLEO.   Sink Rome, and their tongues rot
    That speak against us! A charge we bear i' the war,
    And, as the president of my kingdom, will
    Appear there for a man. Speak not against it;
    I will not stay behind.
ENO.   Nay, I have done.
    Here comes the emperor.

Enter ANTONY *and* CANIDIUS

ANT.   Is it not strange, Canidius,
    That from Tarentum and Brundusium
    He could so quickly cut the Ionian sea,
    And take in Toryne?[4] You have heard on 't, sweet?

---

1. *forspoke*] gainsaid, argued against.
2. *merely*] entirely.
3. *puzzle*] distract.
4. *take in Toryne*] conquer Toryne. Toryne was a small town in Epirus, near Actium.

CLEO.   Celerity is never more admired
　　　Than by the negligent.
ANT.   A good rebuke,
　　　Which might have well becomed the best of men,
　　　To taunt at slackness.[5] Canidius, we
　　　Will fight with him by sea.
CLEO.   By sea: what else?
CAN.   Why will my lord do so?
ANT.   For that he dares us to 't.
ENO.   So hath my lord dared him to single fight.
CAN.   Ay, and to wage this battle at Pharsalia,
　　　Where Cæsar fought with Pompey: but these offers,
　　　Which serve not for his vantage, he shakes off,
　　　And so should you.
ENO.   Your ships are not well mann'd,
　　　Your mariners are muleters, reapers, people
　　　Ingross'd by swift impress;[6] in Cæsar's fleet
　　　Are those that often have 'gainst Pompey fought:
　　　Their ships are yare,[7] yours heavy: no disgrace
　　　Shall fall you for refusing him at sea,
　　　Being prepared for land.
ANT.   By sea, by sea.
ENO.   Most worthy sir, you therein throw away
　　　The absolute soldiership you have by land,
　　　Distract your army, which doth most consist
　　　Of war-mark'd footmen, leave unexecuted
　　　Your own renowned knowledge, quite forgo
　　　The way which promises assurance, and
　　　Give up yourself merely to chance and hazard
　　　From firm security.
ANT.   I 'll fight at sea.
CLEO.   I have sixty sails, Cæsar none better.
ANT.   Our overplus of shipping will we burn;
　　　And, with the rest full-mann'd, from the head of Actium
　　　Beat the approaching Cæsar. But if we fail,
　　　We then can do 't at land.

Enter a Messenger

5. *To taunt at slackness*] in taunting or upbraiding sloth.
6. *Ingross'd by swift impress*] enrolled hastily by forced impressment.
7. *yare*] taut, manageable.

Thy business?

MESS. The news is true, my lord; he is descried;
Cæsar has taken Toryne.

ANT. Can he be there in person? 'tis impossible;
Strange that his power should be. Canidius,
Our nineteen legions thou shalt hold by land,
And our twelve thousand horse. We 'll to our ship:
Away, my Thetis![8]

Enter a Soldier

How now, worthy soldier?

Still his head is turned

SOLD. O noble emperor, do not fight by sea;
Trust not to rotten planks. Do you misdoubt
This sword and these my wounds? Let the Egyptians
And the Phœnicians go a-ducking: we
Have used to conquer, standing on the earth
And fighting foot to foot.

ANT.   Well, well: away!
         [*Exeunt Antony, Cleopatra, and Enobarbus.*

SOLD. By Hercules, I think I am i' the right.

CAN. Soldier, thou art: but his whole action grows
Not in the power on 't:[9] so our leader 's led,
And we are women's men.   → *led by women*

SOLD.   You keep by land
The legions and the horse whole, do you not?

CAN. Marcus Octavius, Marcus Justeius,
Publicola and Cælius, are for sea:
But we keep whole by land. This speed of Cæsar's
Carries beyond belief.

SOLD.   While he was yet in Rome,
His power went out in such distractions[10] as
Beguiled all spies.

CAN.   Who 's his lieutenant, hear you?

SOLD. They say, one Taurus.

CAN.   Well I know the man.

---

8. *Thetis*] a sea-nymph, mother of Achilles.
9. *his . . . on 't*] his whole conduct in the war has not been founded on his greatest
   strength, his land force.
10. *distractions*] separate detachments.

Enter a Messenger

MESS.   The emperor calls Canidius.
CAN.   With news the time's with labour, and throes forth[11]
    Each minute some.   [*Exeunt.*

SCENE VIII. A *Plain near Actium.*

Enter CÆSAR, *and* TAURUS, *with his army, marching*

CÆS.   Taurus!
TAUR.   My lord?
CÆS.   Strike not by land; keep whole: provoke not battle,
    Till we have done at sea. Do not exceed
    The prescript[1] of this scroll: our fortune lies
    Upon this jump.[2]   [*Exeunt.*

SCENE IX. *Another Part of the Plain.*

Enter ANTONY *and* ENOBARBUS

ANT.   Set we our squadrons on yond side o' the hill,
    In eye of Cæsar's battle; from which place
    We may the number of the ships behold,
    And so proceed accordingly.   [*Exeunt.*

---

11. *throes forth*] gives birth to.

---

1. *prescript*] direction, order.
2. *jump*] hazard.

SCENE X. *Another Part of the Plain.*

Enter CANIDIUS, *marching with his land army one way; and* TAURUS, *the lieutenant of* CÆSAR, *with his army, the other way. After their going in, is heard the noise of a sea-fight*

Alarum. Enter ENOBARBUS

ENO.   Naught, naught, all naught! I can behold no longer!
The Antoniad,[1] the Egyptian admiral,
With all their sixty, fly and turn the rudder:
To see 't mine eyes are blasted.

Enter SCARUS

SCAR.   Gods and goddesses,
All the whole synod of them!
ENO.   What's thy passion?
SCAR.   The greater cantle[2] of the world is lost
With very ignorance; we have kiss'd away
Kingdoms and provinces.
ENO.   How appears the fight?
SCAR.   On our side like the token'd pestilence,[3]
Where death is sure. Yon ribaudred nag[4] of Egypt—
Whom leprosy o'ertake!—i' the midst o' the fight,
When vantage[5] like a pair of twins appear'd,
Both as the same, or rather ours the elder,—
The breese[6] upon her, like a cow in June!—
Hoists sails and flies.
ENO.   That I beheld:
Mine eyes did sicken at the sight, and could not
Endure a further view.
SCAR.   She once being loof'd,[7]

1. *Antoniad*] According to North's "Plutarch," the admiral galley of Cleopatra's fleet was named "Antoniad."
2. *cantle*] piece, corner.
3. *the token'd pestilence*] the plague which was always fatal when it developed on the skin certain spots which were popularly called "God's tokens."
4. *ribaudred nag*] obscene strumpet.
5. *vantage*] advantage.
6. *breese*] gadfly, with the obvious pun on "breeze."
7. *loof'd*] luffed, brought close before the wind.

The noble ruin of her magic, Antony,
Claps on his sea-wing, and like a doting mallard,
Leaving the fight in height, flies after her:
I never saw an action of such shame;
Experience, manhood, honour, ne'er before
Did violate so itself.

ENO.   Alack, alack!

Enter CANIDIUS

— Personification

CAN.   Our fortune on the sea is out of breath,
And sinks most lamentably. Had our general
Been what he knew himself, it had gone well:
O, he has given example for our flight   *— by example lieuts*
Most grossly by his own!   *leave.*

ENO.   Ay, are you thereabouts?[8] Why then good night
Indeed.

CAN.   Toward Peloponnesus are they fled.

SCAR.   'Tis easy to 't;[9] and there I will attend
What further comes.

CAN.   To Cæsar will I render
My legions and my horse: six kings already
Show me the way of yielding.

ENO.   I'll yet follow
The wounded chance of Antony, though my reason
Sits in the wind against me.   [*Exeunt.*

SCENE XI. *Alexandria. Cleopatra's Palace.*

Enter ANTONY *with* Attendants

ANT.   Hark! the land bids me tread no more upon 't;
        It is ashamed to bear me. Friends, come hither:
        I am so lated[1] in the world that I

---

8. *are you thereabouts*] is that what you are considering?
9. *'Tis easy to 't*] The voyage to Peloponnesus is easy.

---

1. *lated*] belated, benighted.

Have lost my way for ever. I have a ship
Laden with gold; take that, divide it; fly,
And make your peace with Cæsar.

ALL.　　　　　　　　　　　　Fly! not we.

ANT.　I have fled myself, and have instructed cowards
To run and show their shoulders. Friends, be gone;
I have myself resolved upon a course
Which has no need of you; be gone:
My treasure's in the harbour, take it. O,
I follow'd that I blush to look upon:
My very hairs do mutiny, for the white
Reprove the brown for rashness, and they them
For fear and doting. Friends, be gone: you shall
Have letters from me to some friends that will
Sweep your way for you.[2] Pray you, look not sad,
Nor make replies of loathness:[3] take the hint
Which my despair proclaims; let that be left
Which leaves itself: to the sea-side straightway:
I will possess you of that ship and treasure.
Leave me, I pray, a little: pray you now:
Nay, do so; for indeed I have lost command,[4]
Therefore I pray you: I'll see you by and by.　　　　　[*Sits down.*

Enter CLEOPATRA *led by* CHARMIAN *and* IRAS; EROS *following*

EROS.　Nay, gentle madam, to him, comfort him.

IRAS.　Do, most dear queen.

CHAR.　Do! why, what else?

CLEO.　Let me sit down. O Juno!

ANT.　No, no, no, no, no.

EROS.　See you here, sir?

ANT.　O fie, fie, fie!

CHAR.　Madam!

IRAS.　Madam, O good empress!

EROS.　Sir, sir!

ANT.　Yes, my lord, yes; he at Philippi kept
His sword e'en like a dancer;[5] while I struck

---

2. *Sweep your way for you*] make your way easy for you.
3. *loathness*] reluctance to obey.
4. *I have lost command*] I have lost control of my emotions.

The lean and wrinkled Cassius; and 'twas I
That the mad Brutus ended: he alone
Dealt on lieutenantry[6] and no practice had
In the brave squares of war: yet now—No matter.

CLEO.   Ah! stand by.

EROS.   The queen, my lord, the queen.

IRAS.   Go to him, madam, speak to him:
He is unqualitied[7] with very shame.

CLEO.   Well then, sustain me: O!

EROS.   Most noble sir, arise; the queen approaches:
Her head's declined, and death will seize her, but
Your comfort makes the rescue.

ANT.   I have offended reputation,
A most unnoble swerving.

EROS.   Sir, the queen.

ANT.   O, whither hast thou led me, Egypt? See,
How I convey my shame out of thine eyes
By looking back what I have left behind
Stroy'd in dishonour.[8]

CLEO.   O my lord, my lord,
Forgive my fearful sails! I little thought
You would have follow'd.

ANT.   Egypt, thou knew'st too well
My heart was to thy rudder tied by the strings,
And thou shouldst tow me after: o'er my spirit
Thy full supremacy thou knew'st, and that
Thy beck might from the bidding of the gods
Command me.

CLEO.   O, my pardon!

ANT.   Now I must
To the young man send humble treaties,[9] dodge
And palter[10] in the shifts of lowness; who

---

5. *sword . . . dancer*] seems to allude to the ornamental wearing of a sword, as by a
   dancer.
6. *Dealt on lieutenantry*] fought by proxy, through his subordinates.
7. *unqualitied*] deprived of his faculties (as a soldier).
8. *See . . . dishonour*] See how I avert my eyes from thine and reflect upon the reputation I abandoned with my fleet, destroyed in dishonor.
9. *treaties*] proposals of peace.
10. *palter*] equivocate.

With half the bulk o' the world play'd as I pleased,
Making and marring fortunes. You did know
How much you were my conqueror, and that
My sword, made weak by my affection, would
Obey it on all cause.

CLEO.　　　　　　　Pardon, pardon!

ANT.　Fall not a tear, I say; one of them rates[11]
All that is won and lost: give me a kiss;
Even this repays me. We sent our schoolmaster;[12]
Is he come back? Love, I am full of lead.
Some wine, within there, and our viands! Fortune knows
We scorn her most when most she offers blows.　　　　[*Exeunt.*

SCENE XII. *Egypt. Cæsar's Camp.*

Enter CÆSAR, DOLABELLA, THYREUS, *with others*

CÆS.　Let him appear that's come from Antony.
Know you him?

DOL.　　　　　　Cæsar, 'tis his schoolmaster:
An argument that he is pluck'd, when hither
He sends so poor a pinion of his wing,
Which had superfluous kings for messengers
Not many moons gone by.

Enter EUPHRONIUS, *ambassador from Antony*

CÆS.　　　　　　　　　Approach, and speak.

EUPH.　Such as I am I come from Antony:
I was of late as petty to his ends
As is the morn-dew on the myrtle-leaf
To his grand sea.[1]

---

11. *rates*] pays for, is worth.
12. *our schoolmaster*] Historically the tutor to Antony's children by Cleopatra was Euphronius.

---

1. *To his grand sea*] compared to the full tide of his prosperity.

CÆS.   Be 't so: declare thine office.
EUPH.   Lord of his fortunes he salutes thee, and
     Requires to live in Egypt: which not granted,
     He lessens his requests, and to thee sues
     To let him breathe between the heavens and earth,
     A private man in Athens: this for him.
     Next, Cleopatra does confess thy greatness;
     Submits her to thy might, and of thee craves
     The circle[2] of the Ptolemies for her heirs,
     Now hazarded to thy grace.
CÆS.   For Antony,
     I have no ears to his request. The queen
     Of audience nor desire shall fail, so she
     From Egypt drive her all-disgraced friend,
     Or take his life there: this if she perform,
     She shall not sue unheard. So to them both.
EUPH.   Fortune pursue thee!
CÆS.   Bring him through the bands.
                               [*Exit Euphronius.*
     [*To Thyreus*] To try thy eloquence, now 't is time: dispatch;
     From Antony win Cleopatra: promise,
     And in our name, what she requires; add more,
     From thine invention, offers: women are not
     In their best fortunes strong, but want will perjure
     The ne'er-touch'd vestal: try thy cunning, Thyreus;
     Make thine own edict for thy pains,[3] which we
     Will answer as a law.
THYR.   Cæsar, I go.
CÆS.   Observe how Antony becomes his flaw,[4]
     And what thou think'st his very action speaks
     In every power that moves.[5]
THYR.   Cæsar, I shall.   [*Exeunt.*

---

2. *circle*] crown.
3. *Make . . . pains*] fix the terms of thine own reward for thy trouble.
4. *how . . . flaw*] how Antony bears his misfortunes.
5. *what . . . moves*] what meaning you attach to the slightest movement in all his bearing and gait.

SCENE XIII. *Alexandria. Cleopatra's Palace.*

Enter CLEOPATRA, ENOBARBUS, CHARMIAN, *and* IRAS

CLEO.   What shall we do, Enobarbus?
ENO.   Think, and die.
CLEO.   Is Antony or we in fault for this?
ENO.   Antony only, that would make his will
     Lord of his reason. What though you fled
     From that great face of war, whose several ranges[1]
     Frighted each other, why should he follow?
     The itch of his affection should not then
     Have nick'd his captainship; at such a point,
     When half to half the world opposed, he being
     The mered question:[2] 'twas a shame no less
     Than was his loss, to course[3] your flying flags
     And leave his navy gazing.
CLEO.   Prithee, peace.

Enter ANTONY, *with* EUPHRONIUS *the Ambassador*

ANT.   Is that his answer?
EUPH.   Ay, my lord.
ANT.   The queen shall then have courtesy, so she
     Will yield us up.
EUPH.   He says so.
ANT.   Let her know 't.
     To the boy Cæsar send this grizzled head,
     And he will fill thy wishes to the brim
     With principalities.
CLEO.   That head, my lord?
ANT.   To him again: tell him he wears the rose
     Of youth upon him, from which the world should note
     Something particular: his coin, ships, legions,
     May be a coward's, whose ministers would prevail
     Under the service of a child as soon
     As i' the command of Cæsar: I dare him therefore

---

1. *ranges*] ranks or lines (of ships).
2. *mered question*] sole moving spirit.
3. *course*] pursue.

To lay his gay comparisons[4] apart
And answer me declined,[5] sword against sword,
Ourselves alone. I 'll write it: follow me.

[Exeunt Antony and Euphronius.

ENO.   [*Aside*] Yes, like enough, high-battled Cæsar will
Unstate his happiness[6] and be staged to the show
Against a sworder! I see men's judgements are
A parcel of [7] their fortunes, and things outward
Do draw the inward quality after them,
To suffer all alike. That he should dream,
Knowing all measures, the full Cæsar will
Answer his emptiness! Cæsar, thou hast subdued
His judgement too.

Enter an Attendant

ATT.   A messenger from Cæsar.
CLEO.   What, no more ceremony? See, my women,
Against the blown rose[8] may they stop their nose
That kneel'd unto the buds. Admit him, sir.   *[Exit Attend.*
ENO.   [*Aside*] Mine honesty and I begin to square.[9]
The loyalty well held[10] to fools does make
Our faith mere folly: yet he that can endure
To follow with allegiance a fall'n lord
Does conquer him that did his master conquer,
And earns a place i' the story.

Enter THYREUS

CLEO.   Cæsar's will?
THYR.   Hear it apart.
CLEO.   None but friends: say boldly.
THYR.   So, haply, are they friends to Antony.
ENO.   He needs as many, sir, as Cæsar has,
Or needs not us. If Cæsar please, our master
Will leap to be his friend: for us, you know,

4. *gay comparisons*] comparative advantages.
5. *declined*] in my fallen state.
6. *Unstate his happiness*] abdicate his good fortune.
7. *A parcel of*] of a piece with.
8. *blown rose*] overblown rose, one that has done blossoming.
9. *square*] quarrel.
10. *well held*] kept.

Whose he is we are, and that is Cæsar's.[11]

THYR.   So.
    Thus then, thou most renown'd: Cæsar entreats
    Not to consider in what case thou stand'st
    Further than he is Cæsar.[12]

CLEO.   Go on: right royal.

THYR.   He knows that you embrace not Antony
    As you did love, but as you fear'd him.

CLEO.   O!

THYR.   The scars upon your honour therefore he
    Does pity as constrained blemishes,
    Not as deserved.

CLEO.   He is a god and knows
    What is most right: mine honour was not yielded,
    But conquer'd merely.

ENO.   [*Aside*] To be sure of that,
    I will ask Antony. Sir, sir, thou art so leaky
    That we must leave thee to thy sinking, for
    Thy dearest quit thee.   [*Exit.*

THYR.   Shall I say to Cæsar
    What you require of him? for he partly begs
    To be desired to give. It much would please him,
    That of his fortunes you should make a staff
    To lean upon: but it would warm his spirits,
    To hear from me you had left Antony,
    And put yourself under his shrowd,
    The universal landlord.

CLEO.   What's your name?

THYR.   My name is Thyreus.

CLEO.   Most kind messenger,
    Say to great Cæsar this: in deputation
    I kiss his conquering hand: tell him, I am prompt
    To lay my crown at 's feet, and there to kneel:
    Tell him, from his all-obeying[13] breath I hear
    The doom of Egypt.

THYR.   'Tis your noblest course.

---

11. *Whose . . . Cæsar's*] i.e., whoever rules Antony—and that is Cæsar—rules us as well.

12. *he is Cæsar*] he, being Cæsar, is great enough to be merciful.

13. *all-obeying*] all-obeyed.

    Wisdom and fortune combating together,
    If that the former dare but what it can,
    No chance may shake it. Give me grace to lay
    My duty on your hand.
CLEO.   Your Cæsar's father oft,
    When he hath mused of taking kingdoms in,
    Bestow'd his lips on that unworthy place,
    As[14] it rain'd kisses.

Re-enter ANTONY *and* ENOBARBUS

ANT.   Favours, by Jove that thunders!
    What art thou, fellow?
THYR.   One that but performs
    The bidding of the fullest[15] man and worthiest
    To have command obey'd.
ENO.   [*Aside*] You will be whipp'd.
ANT.   Approach, there! Ah, you kite! Now, gods and devils!
    Authority melts from me: of late, when I cried "Ho!"
    Like boys unto a muss,[16] kings would start forth,
    And cry "Your will?" Have you no ears?
    I am Antony yet.

Enter Attendants

               Take hence this Jack,[17] and whip him.
ENO.   [*Aside*] 'T is better playing with a lion's whelp
    Than with an old one dying.
ANT.   Moon and stars!
    Whip him. Were 't twenty of the greatest tributaries
    That do acknowledge Cæsar, should I find them
    So saucy with the hand of she here,—what's her name,
    Since she was Cleopatra? Whip him, fellows,
    Till, like a boy, you see him cringe his face,
    And whine aloud for mercy: take him hence.
THYR.   Mark Antony,—
ANT.   Tug him away: being whipp'd,
    Bring him again: this Jack of Cæsar's shall

14. *As*] as if.
15. *fullest*] most perfectly endowed.
16. *a muss*] a scramble.
17. *Jack*] a common term of contempt for a saucy fellow.

Bear us an errand to him.   [*Exeunt Attendants, with Thyreus.*
You were half blasted ere I knew you: ha!
Have I my pillow left unpress'd in Rome,
Forborne the getting of a lawful race,
And by a gem of women, to be abused
By one that looks on feeders?[18]

CLEO.   Good my lord,—

ANT.   You have been a boggler[19] ever:
But when we in our viciousness grow hard—
O misery on 't!—the wise gods seel[20] our eyes;
In our own filth drop our clear judgements; make us
Adore our errors; laugh at 's while we strut
To our confusion.

CLEO.   O, is 't come to this?

ANT.   I found you as a morsel cold upon
Dead Cæsar's trencher; nay, you were a fragment[21]
Of Cneius Pompey's; besides what hotter hours,
Unregister'd in vulgar fame,[22] you have
Luxuriously[23] pick'd out: for I am sure,
Though you can guess what temperance should be,
You know not what it is.

CLEO.   Wherefore is this?

ANT.   To let a fellow that will take rewards
And say "God quit[24] you!" be familiar with
My playfellow, your hand, this kingly seal
And plighter of high hearts! O, that I were
Upon the hill of Basan,[25] to outroar
The horned herd! for I have savage cause;
And to proclaim it civilly, were like
A halter'd neck which does the hangman thank
For being yare about him.

Re-enter Attendants, *with* THYREUS

18. *feeders*] servants.
19. *boggler*] inconstant woman.
20. *seel*] sew up, blind; a term of falconry.
21. *fragment*] scrap, poor remnant.
22. *vulgar fame*] popular report.
23. *Luxuriously*] lasciviously, lustfully.
24. *quit*] requite, repay.
25. *the hill of Basan*] a scriptural reference. Cf. *Psalms* 22:12 and 68:15. Antony's likening of himself to a horned beast reflects his belief that he has been cuckolded.

                    Is he whipp'd?

FIRST ATT.   Soundly, my lord.

ANT.   Cried he? and begg'd he pardon?

FIRST ATT.   He did ask favour.

ANT.   If that thy father live, let him repent
    Thou wast not made his daughter; and be thou sorry
    To follow Cæsar in his triumph, since
    Thou hast been whipp'd for following him: henceforth
    The white hand of a lady fever thee,
    Shake thou to look on 't. Get thee back to Cæsar,
    Tell him thy entertainment: look thou say
    He makes me angry with him; for he seems
    Proud and disdainful, harping on what I am,
    Not what he knew I was: he makes me angry;
    And at this time most easy 't is to do 't,
    When my good stars that were my former guides
    Have empty left their orbs[26] and shot their fires
    Into the abysm of hell. If he mislike
    My speech and what is done, tell him he has
    Hipparchus, my enfranched bondman, whom
    He may at pleasure whip, or hang, or torture,
    As he shall like, to quit me: urge it thou:
    Hence with thy stripes, begone!   *[Exit Thyreus.*

CLEO.   Have you done yet?

ANT.   Alack, our terrene moon[27]
    Is now eclipsed, and it portends alone
    The fall of Antony.

CLEO.   I must stay his time.

ANT.   To flatter Cæsar, would you mingle eyes
    With one that ties his points?[28]

CLEO.   Not know me yet?

ANT.   Cold-hearted toward me?

CLEO.   Ah, dear, if I be so,
    From my cold heart let heaven engender hail,
    And poison it in the source, and the first stone
    Drop in my neck: as it determines,[29] so

26. *orbs*] spheres.
27. *terrene moon*] earthly moon, i.e. Cleopatra.
28. *one that ties his points*] his valet, who laces up his trunk-hose.
29. *determines*] ends, dissolves.

Dissolve my life! The next Cæsarion smite!
Till by degrees the memory of my womb,[30]
Together with my brave Egyptians all,
By the discandying[31] of this pelleted storm[32]
Lie graveless, till the flies and gnats of Nile
Have buried them for prey!

ANT.   I am satisfied.
Cæsar sits down in Alexandria, where
I will oppose his fate. Our force by land
Hath nobly held; our sever'd navy too
Have knit again, and fleet,[33] threatening most sea-like.
Where hast thou been, my heart? Dost thou hear, lady?
If from the field I shall return once more
To kiss these lips, I will appear in blood;
I and my sword will earn our chronicle:[34]
There's hope in 't yet.

CLEO. That's my brave lord!

ANT. I will be treble-sinew'd, hearted, breath'd,
And fight maliciously: for when mine hours
Were nice[35] and lucky, men did ransom lives
Of me for jests; but now I'll set my teeth,
And send to darkness all that stop me. Come,
Let's have one other gaudy night: call to me
All my sad captains; fill our bowls once more:
Let's mock the midnight bell.

CLEO.   It is my birth-day:
I had thought to have held it poor,[36] but since my lord
Is Antony again, I will be Cleopatra.

ANT. We will yet do well.

CLEO. Call all his noble captains to my lord.

ANT. Do so, we'll speak to them; and to-night I'll force
The wine peep through their scars. Come on, my queen;
There's sap in 't yet. The next time I do fight
I'll make death love me, for I will contend

---

30. *memory of my womb*] offspring.
31. *discandying*] thawing, melting.
32. *pelleted storm*] hailstorm of pellets.
33. *fleet*] sail securely, float.
34. *chronicle*] place in history.
35. *nice*] devoted to trifling pursuits.
36. *held it poor*] kept it without celebration.

Even with his pestilent scythe.   [*Exeunt all but Enobarbus.*
ENO.   Now he'll outstare the lightning. To be furious
    Is to be frighted out of fear; and in that mood
    The dove will peck the estridge;[37] and I see still,
    A diminution in our captain's brain
    Restores his heart: when valour preys on reason,
    It eats the sword it fights with. I will seek
    Some way to leave him.   [*Exit.*

37. *estridge*] goshawk (not the ostrich).

ACT IV.

SCENE I. *Before Alexandria. Cæsar's Camp.*

Enter CÆSAR, AGRIPPA, *and* MÆCENAS, *with his army:* CÆSAR *reading a letter*

CÆS.   He calls me boy, and chides as he had power
    To beat me out of Egypt; my messenger
    He hath whipp'd with rods; dares me to personal combat,
    Cæsar to Antony. Let the old ruffian know
    I have many other ways to die, meantime
    Laugh at his challenge.
MÆC.   Cæsar must think,
    When one so great begins to rage, he 's hunted
    Even to falling. Give him no breath, but now
    Make boot[1] of his distraction. Never anger
    Made good guard for itself.
CÆS.   Let our best heads
    Know that to-morrow the last of many battles
    We mean to fight. Within our files there are,
    Of those that served Mark Antony but late,
    Enough to fetch him in. See it done:
    And feast the army; we have store to do 't,
    And they have earn'd the waste. Poor Antony!   [*Exeunt.*

SCENE II. *Alexandria. Cleopatra's Palace.*

Enter ANTONY, CLEOPATRA, ENOBARBUS, CHARMIAN, IRAS, ALEXAS, *with others*

ANT.   He will not fight with me, Domitius?

boot] advantage.

76

ENO.   No.
ANT.   Why should he not?
ENO.   He thinks, being twenty times of better fortune,
        He is twenty men to one.
ANT.   To-morrow, soldier,
        By sea and land I 'll fight: or I will live,
        Or bathe my dying honour in the blood
        Shall make it live again. Woo 't thou[1] fight well?
ENO.   I 'll strike, and cry "Take all."
ANT.   Well said; come on.
        Call forth my household servants: let 's to-night
        Be bounteous at our meal.

Enter three or four Servitors

                                Give me thy hand,
        Thou hast been rightly honest;—so hast thou;—
        Thou,—and thou,—and thou: you have served me well,
        And kings have been your fellows.
CLEO.   [*Aside to Eno.*] What means this?
ENO.   [*Aside to Cleo.*] 'T is one of those odd tricks which sorrow shoots
        Out of the mind.
ANT.   And thou art honest too.
        I wish I could be made so many men,
        And all of you clapp'd up together in
        An Antony, that I might do you service
        So good as you have done.
SERV.   The gods forbid!
ANT.   Well, my good fellows, wait on me to-night:
        Scant not my cups, and make as much of me
        As when mine empire was your fellow too
        And suffer'd my command.
CLEO.   [*Aside to Eno.*] What does he mean?
ENO.   [*Aside to Cleo.*] To make his followers weep.
ANT.   Tend me to-night;
        May be it is the period[2] of your duty:
        Haply you shall not see me more; or if,
        A mangled shadow: perchance to-morrow

1. *Woo 't thou*] Wilt thou? "Woo 't" is in itself equivalent to "wilt thou"; "thou" is re-
   dundant.
2. *period*] termination.

You 'll serve another master. I look on you
As one that takes his leave. Mine honest friends,
I turn you not away; but, like a master
Married to your good service, stay till death:
Tend me to-night two hours, I ask no more,
And the gods yield³ you for 't!

ENO.   What mean you, sir,
To give them this discomfort? Look, they weep,
And I, an ass, am onion-eyed: for shame,
Transform us not to women.

ANT.   Ho, ho, ho!
Now the witch take me, if I meant it thus!
Grace grow where those drops fall! My hearty friends,
You take me in too dolorous a sense;
For I spake to you for your comfort, did desire you
To burn this night with torches: know, my hearts,
I hope well of to-morrow, and will lead you
Where rather I 'll expect victorious life
Than death and honour. Let 's to supper, come,
And drown consideration.   [*Exeunt.*

SCENE III. *The Same. Before the Palace.*

Enter two Soldiers *to their guard*

FIRST SOLD.   Brother, good night: to-morrow is the day.
SEC. SOLD.   It will determine one way: fare you well.
     Heard you of nothing strange about the streets?
FIRST SOLD.   Nothing. What news?
SEC. SOLD.   Belike 't is but a rumour. Good night to you.
FIRST SOLD.   Well, sir, good night.

Enter two other Soldiers

SEC. SOLD.   Soldiers, have careful watch.
THIRD SOLD.   And you. Good night, good night.

---

3. *yield*] reward.

                 [*They place themselves in every corner of the stage.*

FOURTH SOLD.   Here we: and if to-morrow
    Our navy thrive, I have an absolute hope
    Our landmen will stand up.

THIRD SOLD.   'T is a brave army,
    And full of purpose.   [*Music of hautboys as under the stage.*

FOURTH SOLD.   Peace! what noise?

FIRST SOLD.   List, list!

SEC. SOLD.   Hark!

FIRST SOLD.   Music i' the air.

THIRD SOLD.   Under the earth.

FOURTH SOLD.   It signs[1] well, does it not?

THIRD SOLD.   No.

FIRST SOLD.   Peace, I say!
    What should this mean?

SEC. SOLD.   'T is the god Hercules,[2] whom Antony loved,
    Now leaves him.

FIRST SOLD.   Walk; let 's see if other watchmen
    Do hear what we do.

SEC. SOLD.   How now, masters!

ALL.   [*Speaking together*] How now! How now! Do you hear this?

FIRST SOLD.   Ay; is 't not strange?

THIRD SOLD.   Do you hear, masters? do you hear?

FIRST SOLD.   Follow the noise so far as we have quarter;
    Let 's see how it will give off.

ALL.   Content.[3] 'T is strange.   [*Exeunt.*

SCENE IV. *The Same. A Room in the Palace.*

Enter ANTONY *and* CLEOPATRA, CHARMIAN *and others attending*

ANT.   Eros! mine armour, Eros!

CLEO.   Sleep a little.

---

1. *signs*] bodes.
2. *Hercules*] In Plutarch, the departing god is not Hercules, but Bacchus, to whom Antony was singularly devoted.
3. *Content*] agreed, all right.

ANT.   No, my chuck. Eros, come; mine armour, Eros!

Enter EROS *with armour*

     Come, good fellow, put mine iron on:
     If fortune be not ours to-day, it is
     Because we brave her: come.
CLEO.   Nay, I 'll help too.
     What 's this for?
ANT.   Ah, let be, let be! thou art
     The armourer of my heart: false, false; this, this.
CLEO.   Sooth, la, I 'll help: thus it must be.
ANT.   Well, well;
     We shall thrive now. Seest thou, my good fellow?
     Go put on thy defences.
EROS.   Briefly, sir.
CLEO.   Is not this buckled well?
ANT.   Rarely, rarely:
     He that unbuckles this, till we do please
     To daff't[1] for our repose, shall hear a storm.
     Thou fumblest, Eros: and my queen 's a squire
     More tight at this than thou: dispatch. O love,
     That thou couldst see my wars to-day, and knew'st
     The royal occupation! thou shouldst see
     A workman in 't!

Enter an armed Soldier

                Good morrow to thee; welcome:
     Thou look'st like him that knows a warlike charge:
     To business that we love we rise betime,
     And go to 't with delight.
SOLD.   A thousand, sir,
     Early though 't be, have on their riveted trim,[2]
     And at the port expect you.   [*Shout. Trumpets flourish.*

Enter Captains *and* Soldiers

CAPT.   The morn is fair. Good morrow, general.
ALL.   Good morrow, general.

---

1. *daff't*] doff it, take it off.
2. *riveted trim*] armor.

ANT.   'T is well blown,[3] lads:
This morning, like the spirit of a youth
That means to be of note, begins betimes.
So, so; come, give me that: this way; well said.
Fare thee well, dame, whate'er becomes of me:
This is a soldier's kiss: rebukeable
And worthy shameful check it were, to stand
On more mechanic[4] compliment; I 'll leave thee
Now like a man of steel. You that will fight,
Follow me close; I'll bring you to 't. Adieu.
                         [*Exeunt Antony, Eros, Captains, and Soldiers.*
CHAR.   Please you, retire to your chamber.
CLEO.   Lead me.
He goes forth gallantly. That he and Cæsar might
Determine this great war in single fight!
Then Antony—but now—Well, on.   [*Exeunt.*

SCENE V. *Alexandria. Antony's Camp.*

Trumpets sound. Enter ANTONY *and* EROS; *a* Soldier *meeting them*

SOLD.   The gods make this a happy day to Antony!
ANT.   Would thou and those thy scars had once prevail'd
    To make me fight at land!
SOLD.   Hadst thou done so,
The kings that have revolted and the soldier
That has this morning left thee would have still
Follow'd thy heels.
ANT.   Who's gone this morning?
SOLD.   Who!
One ever near thee: call for Enobarbus,
He shall not hear thee, or from Cæsar's camp
Say "I am none of thine."
ANT.   What say'st thou?

---

3. *'T is well blown*] The day is in full blossom.
4. *mechanic*] common, vulgar.

SOLD.   Sir,
　　He is with Cæsar.
EROS.   Sir, his chests and treasure
　　He has not with him.
ANT.   Is he gone?
SOLD.   Most certain.
ANT.   Go, Eros, send his treasure after; do it;
　　Detain no jot, I charge thee: write to him—
　　I will subscribe—gentle adieus and greetings;
　　Say that I wish he never find more cause
　　To change a master. O, my fortunes have
　　Corrupted honest men! Dispatch. Enobarbus!   [*Exeunt.*

SCENE VI. *Alexandria. Cæsar's Camp.*

Flourish. Enter CÆSAR *with* AGRIPPA, ENOBARBUS, *and others*

CÆS.   Go forth, Agrippa, and begin the fight:
　　Our will is Antony be took alive;
　　Make it so known.
AGR.   Cæsar, I shall.   [*Exit.*
CÆS.   The time of universal peace is near:
　　Prove this a prosperous day, the three-nook'd[1] world
　　Shall bear the olive freely.

Enter a Messenger

MESS.   Antony
　　Is come into the field.
CÆS.   Go charge Agrippa
　　Plant those that have revolted in the van,
　　That Antony may seem to spend his fury
　　Upon himself.   [*Exeunt all but Enobarbus.*
ENO.   Alexas did revolt, and went to Jewry
　　On affairs of Antony; there did persuade

---

1. *three-nook'd world*] three-cornered world, three regions of the world (Europe, Asia, and Africa).

Great Herod to incline himself to Cæsar
And leave his master Antony: for this pains
Cæsar hath hang'd him. Canidius and the rest
That fell away have entertainment,[2] but
No honourable trust. I have done ill;
Of which I do accuse myself so sorely
That I will joy no more.

Enter a Soldier *of Cæsar's*

SOLD.   Enobarbus, Antony
    Hath after thee sent all thy treasure, with
    His bounty overplus: the messenger
    Came on my guard, and at thy tent is now
    Unloading of his mules.
ENO.   I give it you.
SOLD.   Mock not, Enobarbus:
    I tell you true: best you safed[3] the bringer
    Out of the host; I must attend mine office,
    Or would have done 't myself. Your emperor
    Continues still a Jove.   [*Exit.*
ENO.   I am alone the villain of the earth,
    And feel I am so most. O Antony,
    Thou mine of bounty, how wouldst thou have paid
    My better service, when my turpitude
    Thou dost so crown with gold! This blows my heart:[4]
    If swift thought break it not, a swifter mean
    Shall outstrike thought: but thought will do 't, I feel.
    I fight against thee! No: I will go seek
    Some ditch wherein to die; the foul'st best fits
    My latter part of life.   [*Exit.*

2. *entertainment*] employment and pay.
3. *safed*] safeguarded.
4. *blows my heart*] causes my heart to swell to bursting.

SCENE VII. *Field of Battle between the Camps.*

Alarum. Drums and trumpets. Enter AGRIPPA *and others*

AGR.   Retire, we have engaged ourselves too far:
          Cæsar himself has work, and our oppression[1]
          Exceeds what we expected.   [*Exeunt.*

Alarums. Enter ANTONY, *and* SCARUS *wounded*

SCAR.   O my brave emperor, this is fought indeed!
          Had we done so at first, we had droven them home
          With clouts[2] about their heads.
ANT.   Thou bleed'st apace.
SCAR.   I had a wound here that was like a T,
          But now 't is made an H.[3]   [*Retreat afar off.*
ANT.   They do retire.
SCAR.   We'll beat 'em into bench-holes:[4] I have yet
          Room for six scotches[5] more.

Enter EROS

EROS.   They are beaten, sir, and our advantage serves
          For a fair victory.
SCAR.   Let us score their backs
          And snatch 'em up, as we take hares, behind:
          'T is sport to maul a runner.
ANT.   I will reward thee
          Once for thy spritely comfort, and ten-fold
          For thy good valour. Come thee on.
SCAR.   I'll halt after.   [*Exeunt.*

---

1. *oppression*] difficulty.
2. *clouts*] bandages.
3. *an H*] The pronunciation of the word "ache" was the same as the letter "H," i.e., aitch.
4. *beat 'em into bench-holes*] make 'em take refuge in a privy.
5. *scotches*] slashes, cuts.

SCENE VIII. *Under the Walls of Alexandria.*

Alarum. Enter ANTONY, *in a march*; SCARUS, *with others*

ANT.   We have beat him to his camp: run one before,
And let the queen know of our gests.[1] To-morrow,
Before the sun shall see 's, we'll spill the blood
That has to-day escaped. I thank you all;
For doughty-handed are you, and have fought
Not as you served the cause, but as 't had been
Each man's like mine; you have shown all Hectors.
Enter the city, clip[2] your wives, your friends,
Tell them your feats, whilst they with joyful tears
Wash the congealment from your wounds and kiss
The honour'd gashes whole. [*To Scarus*] Give me thy hand;

Enter CLEOPATRA, *attended*

To this great fairy I'll commend thy acts,
Make her thanks bless thee. O thou day o' the world,
Chain mine arm'd neck; leap thou, attire and all,
Through proof of harness[3] to my heart, and there
Ride on the pants[4] triumphing!
CLEO.   Lord of lords!
O infinite virtue, comest thou smiling from
The world's great snare uncaught?
ANT.   My nightingale,
We have beat them to their beds. What, girl! though grey
Do something mingle with our younger brown, yet ha' we
A brain that nourishes our nerves and can
Get goal for goal of youth.[5] Behold this man;
Commend unto his lips thy favouring hand:
Kiss it, my warrior: he hath fought to-day
As if a god in hate of mankind had
Destroy'd in such a shape.

1. *gests*] feats of arms, exploits.
2. *clip*] embrace.
3. *proof of harness*] proven or tested armor.
4. *pants*] heartbeats.
5. *Get goal for goal of youth*] win as many goals (in a game) as young men.

CLEO.   I'll give thee, friend,
    An armour all of gold; it was a king's.
ANT.   He has deserved it, were it carbuncled
    Like holy Phœbus' car. Give me thy hand:
    Through Alexandria make a jolly march;
    Bear our hack'd targets like[6] the men that owe them:
    Had our great palace the capacity
    To camp this host, we all would sup together
    And drink carouses to the next day's fate,
    Which promises royal peril. Trumpeters,
    With brazen din blast you the city's ear;
    Make mingle with our rattling tabourines;[7]
    That heaven and earth may strike their sounds together,
    Applauding our approach.   [*Exeunt.*

SCENE IX. *Cæsar's Camp.*

Sentinels *at their post*

FIRST SOLD.   If we be not relieved within this hour,
    We must return to the court of guard: the night
    Is shiny, and they say we shall embattle
    By the second hour i' the morn.
SEC. SOLD.   This last day was
    A shrewd[1] one to 's.

Enter ENOBARBUS

ENO.   O, bear me witness, night,—
THIRD SOLD.   What man is this?
SEC. SOLD.   Stand close, and list[2] him.
ENO.   Be witness to me, O thou blessed moon,
    When men revolted shall upon record

---

6. *hack'd targets like*] shields hacked about like.
7. *tabourines*] kettledrums.

---

1. *shrewd*] cursed, disastrous.
2. *list*] listen to.

    Bear hateful memory, poor Enobarbus did
    Before thy face repent!
FIRST SOLD.   Enobarbus!
THIRD SOLD.   Peace!
    Hark further.
ENO.   O sovereign mistress of true melancholy,
    The poisonous damp of night disponge³ upon me,
    That life, a very rebel to my will,
    May hang no longer on me: throw my heart
    Against the flint and hardness of my fault;
    Which, being dried with grief, will break to powder,
    And finish all foul thoughts. O Antony,
    Nobler than my revolt is infamous,
    Forgive me in thine own particular,
    But let the world rank me in register⁴
    A master-leaver and a fugitive:
    O Antony! O Antony!   [*Dies.*
SEC. SOLD.   Let's speak to him.
FIRST SOLD.   Let's hear him, for the things he speaks
    May concern Cæsar.
THIRD SOLD.   Let's do so. But he sleeps.
FIRST SOLD.   Swoons rather; for so bad a prayer as his
    Was never yet for sleep.
SEC. SOLD.   Go we to him.
THIRD SOLD.   Awake, sir, awake; speak to us.
SEC. SOLD.   Hear you, sir?
FIRST SOLD.   The hand of death hath raught⁵ him.
    [*Drums afar off.*] Hark! the drums
    Demurely wake the sleepers. Let us bear him
    To the court of guard; he is of note: our hour
    Is fully out.
THIRD SOLD.   Come on, then; he may recover yet.
                          [*Exeunt with the body.*

---

3. *disponge*] discharge like a squeezed sponge.
4. *rank me in register*] make formal record of me.
5. *raught*] reached.

SCENE X. *Between the Two Camps.*

Enter ANTONY *and* SCARUS, *with their Army*

ANT.   Their preparation is to-day by sea;
  We please them not by land.
SCAR.   For both,[1] my lord.
ANT.   I would they'ld fight i' the fire or i' the air;
  We'ld fight there too. But this it is; our foot
  Upon the hills adjoining to the city
  Shall stay with us: order for sea is given;
  They have put forth the haven . . . . . .[2]
  Where their appointment we may best discover
  And look on their endeavour.   [*Exeunt.*

SCENE XI. *Another Part of the Same.*

Enter CÆSAR, *and his Army*

CÆS.   But being charged,[1] we will be still by land,
  Which, as I take 't, we shall; for his best force
  Is forth to man his galleys. To the vales,
  And hold our best advantage.   [*Exeunt.*

SCENE XII. *Hills Adjoining to Alexandria.*

Enter ANTONY *and* SCARUS

ANT.   Yet they are not join'd: where yond pine does stand,

1. *For both*] both by sea and land.
2. *They . . . haven* . . . . . .] The line is metrically imperfect and probably incomplete.

***

1. *But being charged*] Unless we be charged.

  I shall discover all: I'll bring thee word
  Straight, how 'tis like to go.   [*Exit.*
SCAR.   Swallows have built
  In Cleopatra's sails their nests: the augurers
  Say they know not, they cannot tell; look grimly
  And dare not speak their knowledge. Antony
  Is valiant, and dejected, and by starts
  His fretted fortunes give him hope, and fear,
  Of what he has, and has not. [*Alarum afar off, as at a sea-fight.*

Re-enter ANTONY

ANT.   All is lost;
  This foul Egyptian hath betrayed me:
  My fleet hath yielded to the foe; and yonder
  They cast their caps up and carouse together
  Like friends long lost. Triple-turn'd[1] whore! 'tis thou
  Hast sold me to this novice, and my heart
  Makes only wars on thee. Bid them all fly;
  For when I am revenged upon my charm,[2]
  I have done all. Bid them all fly; begone. [*Exit Scarus.*
  O sun, thy uprise shall I see no more:
  Fortune and Antony part here, even here
  Do we shake hands. All come to this? The hearts
  That spaniel'd[3] me at heels, to whom I gave
  Their wishes, do discandy, melt their sweets
  On blossoming Cæsar; and this pine is bark'd,
  That overtopp'd them all. Betray'd I am.
  O this false soul of Egypt! this grave charm,
  Whose eye beck'd[4] forth my wars and call'd them home,
  Whose bosom was my crownet,[5] my chief end,
  Like a right gipsy hath at fast and loose[6]
  Beguiled me to the very heart of loss.
  What, Eros, Eros!

1. *Triple-turn'd*] thrice faithless (to Julius Cæsar, to Cneius Pompeius, and now to Antony).
2. *my charm*] the woman who has bewitched me.
3. *spaniel'd*] fawned like spaniels.
4. *beck'd*] beckoned.
5. *crownet*] coronet, crown.
6. *fast and loose*] a cheating game, the name of which has become proverbial.

Enter CLEOPATRA

　　　　　　　　　　Ah, thou spell! Avaunt!
CLEO.　Why is my lord enraged against his love?
ANT.　Vanish, or I shall give thee thy deserving,
　　And blemish Cæsar's triumph. Let him take thee,
　　And hoist thee up to the shouting plebeians:
　　Follow his chariot, like the greatest spot[7]
　　Of all thy sex: most monster-like, be shown
　　For poor'st diminutives,[8] for doits;[9] and let
　　Patient Octavia plough thy visage up
　　With her prepared nails.　　　　　[*Exit Cleopatra.*
　　　　　　　　　　'T is well thou 'rt gone,
　　If it be well to live; but better 't were
　　Thou fell'st into my fury, for one death
　　Might have prevented many. Eros, ho!
　　The shirt of Nessus is upon me: teach me,
　　Alcides, thou mine ancestor, thy rage:
　　Let me lodge Lichas on the horns o' the moon,[10]
　　And with those hands that grasp'd the heaviest club
　　Subdue my worthiest self. The witch shall die:
　　To the young Roman boy she hath sold me, and I fall
　　Under this plot: she dies for 't. Eros, ho!　　　　[*Exit.*

SCENE XIII. *Alexandria. Cleopatra's Palace.*

Enter CLEOPATRA, CHARMIAN, IRAS, *and* MARDIAN

CLEO.　Help me, my women! O, he is more mad
　　Than Telamon for his shield;[1] the boar of Thessaly[2]
　　Was never so emboss'd.[3]

　7.　*spot*] defilement, disgrace.
　8.　*diminutives*] insignificant creatures, i.e., the rabble.
　9.　*doits*] very small coins.
10.　*The shirt . . . moon*] Fatally wounded whilst trying to rape Hercules' wife, the cen-
　　taur Nessus vengefully gave his poison-soaked shirt to her as a supposed love-charm
　　for her husband. Hercules in his dying agonies threw his page Lichas, who had
　　brought him the garment, high into the air.

CHAR.   To the monument!
    There lock yourself, and send him word you are dead.
    The soul and body rive[4] not more in parting
    Than greatness going off.
CLEO.   To the monument!
    Mardian, go tell him I have slain myself;
    Say that the last I spoke was "Antony,"
    And word it, prithee, piteously: hence, Mardian,
    And bring me how he takes my death. To the monument!
                           [*Exeunt.*

SCENE XIV. *The Same. Another Room.*

Enter ANTONY *and* EROS

ANT.   Eros, thou yet behold'st me?
EROS.   Ay, noble lord.
ANT.   Sometime we see a cloud that 's dragonish,[1]
    A vapour sometime like a bear or lion,
    A tower'd citadel, a pendent rock,
    A forked mountain, or blue promontory
    With trees upon 't, that nod unto the world,
    And mock our eyes with air: thou hast seen these signs;
    They are black vesper's pageants.
EROS.   Ay, my lord.
ANT.   That which is now a horse, even with a thought
    The rack dislimns[2] and makes it indistinct

---

1. *Telamon for his shield*] Ajax, the son of Telamon, went mad and killed himself
   when the shield of Achilles was awarded to Odysseus and not him.
2. *the boar of Thessaly*] the boar sent by Diana to ravage Calydon, which was
   slain by Meleager.
3. *emboss'd*] flecked with foam, as an animal in the chase.
4. *rive*] split asunder.

---

1. *dragonish*] shaped like a dragon.
2. *the rack dislimns*] the cloud blots or effaces (it).

    As water is in water.

EROS.   It does, my lord.

ANT.   My good knave Eros, now thy captain is
    Even such a body: here I am Antony,
    Yet cannot hold this visible shape, my knave.
    I made these wars for Egypt; and the queen—
    Whose heart I thought I had, for she had mine,
    Which, whilst it was mine, had annex'd unto 't
    A million moe, now lost,—she, Eros, has
    Pack'd cards[3] with Cæsar, and false-play'd my glory
    Unto an enemy's triumph.
    Nay, weep not, gentle Eros; there is left us
    Ourselves to end ourselves.

Enter MARDIAN

                      O, thy vile lady!
    She has robb'd me of my sword.

MAR.   No, Antony;
    My mistress loved thee, and her fortunes mingled
    With thine entirely.

ANT.   Hence, saucy eunuch; peace!
    She hath betray'd me, and shall die the death.

MAR.   Death of one person can be paid but once,
    And that she has discharged: what thou wouldst do
    Is done unto thy hand: the last she spake
    Was "Antony! most noble Antony!"
    Then in the midst a tearing groan did break
    The name of Antony; it was divided
    Between her heart and lips: she render'd[4] life,
    Thy name so buried in her.

ANT.   Dead then?

MAR.   Dead.

ANT.   Unarm, Eros; the long day's task is done,
    And we must sleep. [*To Mar.*] That thou depart'st hence safe,
    Does pay thy labour richly; go.   [*Exit Mardian.*
                    Off, pluck off:
    The seven-fold shield of Ajax cannot keep
    The battery from my heart. O, cleave, my sides!

3. *Pack'd cards*] fraudulently dealt cards.
4. *render'd*] gave up, yielded.

Heart, once be stronger than thy continent,[5]
Crack thy frail case! Apace, Eros, apace!
No more a soldier. Bruised pieces, go;
You have been nobly borne. From me awhile.   [*Exit Eros.*
I will o'ertake thee, Cleopatra, and
Weep for my pardon. So it must be, for now
All length[6] is torture: since the torch is out,
Lie down and stray no farther: now all labour
Mars what it does; yea, very force entangles
Itself with strength: seal then, and all is done.
Eros!—I come, my queen. Eros!—Stay for me:
Where souls do couch on flowers, we 'll hand in hand,
And with our sprightly port make the ghosts gaze:
Dido and her Æneas shall want troops,[7]
And all the haunt be ours. Come, Eros, Eros!

Re-enter EROS

EROS.   What would my lord?
ANT.   Since Cleopatra died
I have lived in such dishonour that the gods
Detest my baseness. I, that with my sword
Quarter'd the world, and o'er green Neptune's back
With ships made cities, condemn myself to lack
The courage of a woman; less noble mind
Than she which by her death our Cæsar tells
"I am conqueror of myself." Thou art sworn, Eros,
That, when the exigent[8] should come—which now
Is come indeed—when I should see behind me
The inevitable prosecution[9] of
Disgrace and horror, that, on my command,
Thou then wouldst kill me: do 't; the time is come:
Thou strikest not me, 'tis Cæsar thou defeat'st.
Put colour in thy cheek.
EROS.   The gods withhold me!
Shall I do that which all the Parthian darts,

5. *continent*] container.
6. *length*] perpetuation of life.
7. *Dido . . . troops*] i.e., they shall outshine even Dido and Æneas as the most conspicuous lovers in Elysium.
8. *exigent*] extremity, decisive moment.
9. *prosecution*] pursuit.

Though enemy, lost aim and could not?

ANT.   Eros,
Wouldst thou be window'd[10] in great Rome, and see
Thy master thus with pleach'd[11] arms, bending down
His corrigible[12] neck, his face subdued
To penetrative shame, whilst the wheel'd seat
Of fortunate Cæsar, drawn before him, branded
His baseness that ensued?

EROS.   I would not see 't.

ANT.   Come, then; for with a wound I must be cured.
Draw that thy honest sword, which thou hast worn
Most useful for thy country.

EROS.   O, sir, pardon me!

ANT.   When I did make thee free, sworest thou not then
To do this when I bade thee? Do it at once;
Or thy precedent services are all
But accidents unpurposed. Draw, and come.

EROS.   Turn from me then that noble countenance,
Wherein the worship of the whole world lies.

ANT.   Lo thee!   [*Turning from him.*

EROS.   My sword is drawn.

ANT.   Then let it do at once
The thing why thou hast drawn it.

EROS.   My dear master,
My captain, and my emperor, let me say,
Before I strike this bloody stroke, farewell.

ANT.   'Tis said, man; and farewell.

EROS.   Farewell, great chief. Shall I strike now?

ANT.   Now, Eros.

EROS.   Why, there then: thus I do escape the sorrow
Of Antony's death.   [*Kills himself.*

ANT.   Thrice-nobler than myself!
Thou teachest me, O valiant Eros, what
I should and thou couldst not. My queen and Eros
Have by their brave instruction got upon me[13]
A nobleness in record: but I will be

10. *window'd*] looking from a window.
11. *pleach'd*] folded, intertwined.
12. *corrigible*] subjected to punishment.
13. *got upon me*] gained advantage of me.

A bridegroom in my death, and run into 't
As to a lover's bed. Come then; and, Eros,
Thy master dies thy scholar: to do thus   [*Falling on his sword.*
I learn'd of thee. How! not dead? not dead?
The guard, ho! O, dispatch me!

Enter DERCETAS *and* Guard

FIRST GUARD.   What's the noise?
ANT.   I have done my work ill, friends: O, make an end
    Of what I have begun.
SEC. GUARD.   The star is fall'n.
FIRST GUARD.   And time is at his period.
ALL.   Alas, and woe!
ANT.   Let him that loves me strike me dead.
FIRST GUARD.   Not I.
SEC. GUARD.   Nor I.
THIRD GUARD.   Nor any one.   [*Exeunt Guard.*
DER.   Thy death and fortunes bid thy followers fly.
    This sword but shown to Cæsar, with this tidings,
    Shall enter me with[14] him.

Enter DIOMEDES

DIO.   Where 's Antony?
DER.   There, Diomed, there.
DIO.   Lives he?
    Wilt thou not answer, man?   [*Exit Dercetas.*
ANT.   Art thou there, Diomed? Draw thy sword, and give me
    Sufficing strokes for death.
DIO.   Most absolute lord,
    My mistress Cleopatra sent me to thee.
ANT.   When did she send thee?
DIO.   Now, my lord.
ANT.   Where is she?
DIO.   Lock'd in her monument. She had a prophesying fear
    Of what hath come to pass: for when she saw—
    Which never shall be found—you did suspect
    She had disposed with Cæsar, and that your rage
    Would not be purged, she sent you word she was dead;
    But, fearing since how it might work, hath sent

---

14. *enter me with*] recommend me to.

Me to proclaim the truth; and I am come,
I dread, too late.
ANT. Too late, good Diomed: call my guard, I prithee.
DIO. What, ho, the emperor's guard! The guard, what, ho!
Come, your lord calls.

Enter four or five of the Guard *of Antony*

ANT. Bear me, good friends, where Cleopatra bides;
'T is the last service that I shall command you.
FIRST GUARD. Woe, woe are we, sir, you may not live to wear
All your true followers out.
ALL. Most heavy day!
ANT. Nay, good my fellows, do not please sharp fate
To grace it with your sorrows: bid that welcome
Which comes to punish us, and we punish it
Seeming to bear it lightly. Take me up:
I have led you oft: carry me now, good friends,
And have my thanks for all. [*Exeunt, bearing Antony.*

SCENE XV. *The Same. A Monument.*

Enter CLEOPATRA, *and her maids aloft, with* CHARMIAN, *and* IRAS

CLEO. O Charmian, I will never go from hence.
CHAR. Be comforted, dear madam.
CLEO. No, I will not:
All strange and terrible events are welcome,
But comforts we despise; our size of sorrow,
Proportion'd to our cause, must be as great
As that which makes it.

Enter, below, DIOMEDES

How now! is he dead?
DIO. His death 's upon him, but not dead.
Look out o' the other side your monument;
His guard have brought him thither.

Enter, below, ANTONY, *borne by the* Guard

CLEO.   O sun,
    Burn the great sphere thou movest in! darkling stand
    The varying shore o' the world. O Antony,
    Antony, Antony! Help, Charmian, help, Iras, help;
    Help, friends below; let 's draw him hither.
ANT.   Peace!
    Not Cæsar's valour hath o'erthrown Antony,
    But Antony's hath triumph'd on itself.
CLEO.   So it should be, that none but Antony
    Should conquer Antony; but woe 't is so!
ANT.   I am dying, Egypt, dying; only
    I here importune death awhile, until
    Of many thousand kisses the poor last
    I lay upon thy lips.
CLEO.   I dare not, dear,
    Dear my lord, pardon, I dare not,
    Lest I be taken: not the imperious[1] show
    Of the full-fortuned Cæsar ever shall
    Be brooch'd[2] with me; if knife, drugs, serpents, have
    Edge, sting, or operation, I am safe:
    Your wife Octavia, with her modest eyes
    And still conclusion,[3] shall acquire no honour
    Demuring[4] upon me. But come, come, Antony,—
    Help me, my women,—we must draw thee up;
    Assist, good friends.
ANT.   O, quick, or I am gone.
CLEO.   Here 's sport indeed! How heavy weighs my lord!
    Our strength is all gone into heaviness;
    That makes the weight. Had I great Juno's power,
    The strong-wing'd Mercury should fetch thee up
    And set thee by Jove's side. Yet come a little—
    Wishers were ever fools—O, come, come, come;
                   [They heave Antony aloft to Cleopatra.
    And welcome, welcome! die where thou hast lived:

---

1. *imperious*] imperial.
2. *brooch'd*] ornamented as with a brooch.
3. *still conclusion*] composed judgment.
4. *Demuring*] looking demurely.

Quicken[5] with kissing: had my lips that power,
Thus would I wear them out.
ALL.   A heavy sight!
ANT.   I am dying, Egypt, dying:
Give me some wine, and let me speak a little.
CLEO.   No, let me speak, and let me rail so high,
That the false housewife[6] Fortune break her wheel,
Provoked by my offence.
ANT.   One word, sweet queen:
Of Cæsar seek your honour, with your safety. O!
CLEO.   They do not go together.
ANT.   Gentle, hear me:
None about Cæsar trust but Proculeius.
CLEO.   My resolution and my hands I'll trust;
None about Cæsar.
ANT.   The miserable change now at my end
Lament nor sorrow at, but please your thoughts
In feeding them with those my former fortunes
Wherein I lived, the greatest prince o' the world,
The noblest, and do now not basely die,
Not cowardly put off my helmet to
My countryman, a Roman by a Roman
Valiantly vanquish'd. Now my spirit is going;
I can no more.
CLEO.   Noblest of men, woo 't die?
Hast thou no care of me? shall I abide
In this dull world, which in thy absence is
No better than a sty? O, see, my women,   [*Antony dies.*
The crown o' the earth doth melt. My lord!
O, wither'd is the garland of the war,
The soldier's pole[7] is fall'n: young boys and girls
Are level now with men; the odds[8] is gone,
And there is nothing left remarkable
Beneath the visiting moon.   [*Faints.*
CHAR.   O, quietness, lady!
IRAS.   She's dead too, our sovereign.

5. *Quicken*] revive.
6. *housewife*] "Housewife" is here used contemptuously to mean "hussy."
7. *soldier's pole*] standard, banner.
8. *odds*] inequalities.

CHAR.   Lady!
IRAS.   Madam!
CHAR.   O madam, madam, madam!
IRAS.   Royal Egypt, Empress!
CHAR.   Peace, peace, Iras!
CLEO.   No more, but e'en a woman, and commanded
      By such poor passion as the maid that milks
      And does the meanest chares. It were for me
      To throw my sceptre at the injurious gods,
      To tell them that this world did equal theirs
      Till they had stol'n our jewel. All's but naught;
      Patience is sottish, and impatience does
      Become a dog that's mad: then is it sin
      To rush into the secret house of death,
      Ere death dare come to us? How do you, women?
      What, what! good cheer! Why, how now, Charmian!
      My noble girls! Ah, women, women, look,
      Our lamp is spent, it's out! Good sirs,[9] take heart:
      We'll bury him; and then, what's brave, what's noble,
      Let's do it after the high Roman fashion,
      And make death proud to take us. Come, away:
      This case of that huge spirit now is cold:
      Ah, women, women! Come; we have no friend
      But resolution and the briefest end.
                  [*Exeunt: those above bearing off Antony's body.*

9. *Good sirs*] Cleopatra is still addressing her waiting-women.

ACT V.

SCENE I. *Alexandria. Cæsar's Camp.*

Enter CÆSAR, AGRIPPA, DOLABELLA, MÆCENAS, GALLUS, PROCULEIUS, *and others, his council of war*

CÆS. Go to him, Dolabella, bid him yield;
    Being so frustrate,[1] tell him he mocks
    The pauses that he makes.[2]
DOL.   Cæsar, I shall.   [*Exit.*

Enter DERCETAS, *with the sword of Antony*

CÆS. Wherefore is that? and what art thou that darest
    Appear thus to us?
DER.   I am call'd Dercetas;
    Mark Antony I served, who best was worthy
    Best to be served: whilst he stood up and spoke,
    He was my master, and I wore my life
    To spend upon his haters. If thou please
    To take me to thee, as I was to him
    I'll be to Cæsar; if thou pleasest not,
    I yield thee up my life.
CÆS.   What is 't thou say'st?
DER. I say, O Cæsar, Antony is dead.
CÆS. The breaking of so great a thing should make
    A greater crack: the round world
    Should have shook lions into civil streets,
    And citizens to their dens. The death of Antony
    Is not a single doom;[3] in the name lay
    A moiety of the world.
DER.   He is dead, Cæsar;
    Not by a public minister of justice,
    Nor by a hired knife; but that self hand,

1. *frustrate*] helpless, defeated.
2. *mocks . . . makes*] makes a mockery of himself with his delays.
3. *a single doom*] a death of an individual.

Which writ his honour in the acts it did,
Hath, with the courage which the heart did lend it,
Splitted the heart. This is his sword;
I robb'd his wound of it; behold it stain'd
With his most noble blood.

CÆS.   Look you sad, friends?
The gods rebuke me, but it is tidings
To wash the eyes of kings.

AGR.   And strange it is
That nature must compel us to lament
Our most persisted deeds.

MÆC.   His taints and honours
Waged equal[4] with him.

AGR.   A rarer spirit never
Did steer humanity: but you, gods, will give us
Some faults to make us men. Cæsar is touch'd.

MÆC.   When such a spacious mirror's set before him,
He needs must see himself.

CÆS.   O Antony!
I have follow'd thee to this. But we do lance
Diseases in our bodies: I must perforce
Have shown to thee such a declining day,
Or look on thine; we could not stall together
In the whole world: but yet let me lament,
With tears as sovereign as the blood of hearts,
That thou, my brother, my competitor
In top of all design,[5] my mate in empire,
Friend and companion in the front of war,
The arm of mine own body and the heart
Where mine his thoughts did kindle, that our stars
Unreconciliable should divide
Our equalness to this. Hear me, good friends,—

Enter an Egyptian

But I will tell you at some meeter season:
The business of this man looks out of him;
We'll hear him what he says. Whence are you?

EGYP.   A poor Egyptian yet. The queen my mistress,

---

4. *Waged equal*] equally balanced each other.
5. *my competitor . . . design*] my colleague in all the highest ambitions.

Confined in all she has, her monument,
Of thy intents desires instruction,
That she preparedly may frame herself
To the way she 's forced to.

Cæs.   Bid her have good heart:
She soon shall know of us, by some of ours,
How honourable and how kindly we
Determine for her; for Cæsar cannot live
To be ungentle.

Egyp.   So the gods preserve thee!   [*Exit.*

Cæs.   Come hither, Proculeius. Go and say,
We purpose her no shame: give her what comforts
The quality of her passion shall require,
Lest in her greatness by some mortal stroke
She do defeat us; for her life in Rome
Would be eternal in our triumph:[6] go,
And with your speediest bring us what she says
And how you find of her.

Pro.   Cæsar, I shall.   [*Exit.*

Cæs.   Gallus, go you along. [*Exit Gallus.*] Where 's Dolabella,
To second Proculeius?

All.   Dolabella!

Cæs.   Let him alone, for I remember now
How he 's employ'd: he shall in time be ready.
Go with me to my tent; where you shall see
How hardly I was drawn into this war;
How calm and gentle I proceeded still
In all my writings: go with me, and see
What I can show in this.   [*Exeunt.*

SCENE II. *Alexandria. The Monument.*

Enter CLEOPATRA, CHARMIAN, *and* IRAS

Cleo.   My desolation does begin to make

---

6. *eternal in our triumph*] would live forever in our triumph.

A better life. 'T is paltry to be Cæsar;
Not being Fortune, he 's but Fortune's knave,
A minister of her will: and it is great
To do that thing that ends all other deeds;
Which shackles accidents and bolts up change;
Which sleeps, and never palates more the dug,
The beggar's nurse and Cæsar's.

Enter, to the gates of the monument, PROCULEIUS, GALLUS, *and*
Soldiers

PRO.   Cæsar sends greeting to the Queen of Egypt,
And bids thee study on what fair demands
Thou mean'st to have him grant thee.
CLEO.   What 's thy name?
PRO.   My name is Proculeius.
CLEO.   Antony
Did tell me of you, bade me trust you, but
I do not greatly care to be deceived,
That have no use for trusting. If your master
Would have a queen his beggar, you must tell him,
That majesty, to keep decorum, must
No less beg[1] than a kingdom: if he please
To give me conquer'd Egypt for my son,
He gives me so much of mine own as I
Will kneel to him with thanks.
PRO.   Be of good cheer;
You 're fall'n into a princely hand; fear nothing:
Make your full reference freely to my lord,
Who is so full of grace that it flows over
On all that need. Let me report to him
Your sweet dependency,[2] and you shall find
A conqueror that will pray in aid[3] for kindness,
Where he for grace is kneel'd to.
CLEO.   Pray you, tell him
I am his fortune's vassal and I send him
The greatness he has got.[4] I hourly learn

1. *No less beg*] beg nothing less.
2. *dependency*] submissiveness.
3. *pray in aid*] petition for assistance.
4. *send him . . . got*] acknowledge the supremacy he has got over me.

A doctrine of obedience, and would gladly
Look him i' the face.
PRO.   This I 'll report, dear lady.
Have comfort, for I know your plight is pitied
Of him that caused it.
GAL.   You see how easily she may be surprised.

[*Here Proculeius and two of the Guard ascend the monument by a
ladder placed against a window, and, having descended, come behind Cleopatra. Some of the Guard unbar and open the gates.*[5]

Guard her till Cæsar come.   [*Exit.*
IRAS.   Royal queen!
CHAR.   O Cleopatra! thou art taken, queen!
CLEO.   Quick, quick, good hands.   [*Drawing a dagger.*
PRO.   Hold, worthy lady, hold:
                                [*Seizes and disarms her.*
Do not yourself such wrong, who are in this
Relieved, but not betray'd.
CLEO.   What, of death too,
That rids our dogs of languish?[6]
PRO.   Cleopatra,
Do not abuse my master's bounty by
The undoing of yourself: let the world see
His nobleness well acted, which your death
Will never let come forth.
CLEO.   Where art thou, death?
Come hither, come! come, come, and take a queen
Worth many babes and beggars!
PRO.   O, temperance,[7] lady!
CLEO.   Sir, I will eat no meat, I 'll not drink, sir;
If idle talk will once[8] be necessary,
I 'll not sleep neither: this mortal house I 'll ruin,
Do Cæsar what he can. Know, sir, that I
Will not wait pinion'd at your master's court,
Nor once be chastised with the sober eye

5. *Here . . . gates*] This stage direction, omitted in the Folios, is conjectural. It has been
reconstructed from Plutarch's description of the mode in which Proculeius and his
companions gain entry to the monument.
6. *languish*] protraction of misery.
7. *temperance*] moderation.
8. *once*] at any time.

    Of dull Octavia. Shall they hoist me up
    And show me to the shouting varletry
    Of censuring Rome? Rather a ditch in Egypt
    Be gentle grave unto me! rather on Nilus' mud
    Lay me stark naked, and let the water-flies
    Blow me into abhorring![9] rather make
    My country's high pyramides my gibbet,
    And hang me up in chains!
PRO.   You do extend
    These thoughts of horror further than you shall
    Find cause in Cæsar.

Enter DOLABELLA

DOL.   Proculeius,
    What thou hast done thy master Cæsar knows,
    And he hath sent for thee: for the queen,
    I'll take her to my guard.
PRO.   So, Dolabella,
    It shall content me best: be gentle to her.
    [*To Cleo.*] To Cæsar I will speak what you shall please,
    If you'll employ me[10] to him.
CLEO.   Say, I would die.
                     [*Exeunt Proculeius and Soldiers.*
DOL.   Most noble empress, you have heard of me?
CLEO.   I cannot tell.
DOL.   Assuredly you know me.
CLEO.   No matter, sir, what I have heard or known.
    You laugh when boys or women tell their dreams;
    Is't not your trick?
DOL.   I understand not, madam.
CLEO.   I dream'd there was an emperor Antony:
    O, such another sleep, that I might see
    But such another man!
DOL.   If it might please ye,—
CLEO.   His face was as the heavens; and therein stuck
    A sun and moon, which kept their course and lighted
    The little O, the earth.
DOL.   Most sovereign creature,—

  9. *Blow me into abhorring*] flyblow me into an object of loathing.
10. *employ me*] send me with a commission.

CLEO.   His legs bestrid the ocean: his rear'd arm
     Crested the world: his voice was propertied
     As all the tuned spheres,[11] and that to friends;
     But when he meant to quail[12] and shake the orb,
     He was as rattling thunder. For his bounty,
     There was no winter in 't; an autumn 't was
     That grew the more by reaping: his delights
     Were dolphin-like; they show'd his back above
     The element they lived in: in his livery
     Walk'd crowns and crownets; realms and islands were
     As plates[13] dropp'd from his pocket.
DOL.   Cleopatra,—
CLEO.   Think you there was, or might be, such a man
     As this I dream'd of?
DOL.   Gentle madam, no.
CLEO.   You lie, up to the hearing of the gods.
     But if there be, or ever were, one such,
     It's past the size of dreaming: nature wants stuff
     To vie strange forms with fancy;[14] yet to imagine
     An Antony, were nature's piece 'gainst fancy,
     Condemning shadows quite.
DOL.   Hear me, good madam.
     Your loss is as yourself, great; and you bear it
     As answering to the weight: would I might never
     O'ertake pursued success, but I do feel,[15]
     By the rebound of yours, a grief that smites
     My very heart at root.
CLEO.   I thank you, sir.
     Know you what Cæsar means to do with me?
DOL.   I am loath to tell you what I would you knew.
CLEO.   Nay, pray you, sir,—
DOL.   Though he be honourable,—
CLEO.   He'll lead me then in triumph?
DOL.   Madam, he will; I know 't.
          [*Flourish and shout within:* "Make way there: Cæsar!"

11. *properties . . . spheres*] endowed with all the music of the spheres.
12. *quail*] make tremble, overawe.
13. *plates*] small coins.
14. *nature . . . fancy*] nature lacks the material to equal fancy in framing unwonted
    shapes.
15. *but I do feel*] if I do not feel.

Enter CÆSAR, GALLUS, PROCULEIUS, MÆCENAS, SELEUCUS, *and others of his Train*

CÆS.   Which is the Queen of Egypt?
DOL.   It is the emperor, madam.   [*Cleopatra kneels.*
CÆS.   Arise, you shall not kneel:
    I pray you, rise; rise, Egypt.
CLEO.   Sir, the gods
    Will have it thus; my master and my lord
    I must obey.
CÆS.   Take to you no hard thoughts:
    The record of what injuries you did us,
    Though written in our flesh, we shall remember
    As things but done by chance.
CLEO.   Sole sir o' the world,
    I cannot project mine own cause so well
    To make it clear; but do confess I have
    Been laden with like frailties which before
    Have often shamed our sex.
CÆS.   Cleopatra, know,
    We will extenuate rather than enforce:[16]
    If you apply yourself to our intents,
    Which towards you are most gentle, you shall find
    A benefit in this change; but if you seek
    To lay on me a cruelty by taking
    Antony's course, you shall bereave yourself
    Of my good purposes and put your children
    To that destruction which I'll guard them from
    If thereon you rely. I'll take my leave.
CLEO.   And may, through all the world: 'tis yours; and we,
    Your scutcheons and your signs of conquest, shall
    Hang in what place you please. Here, my good lord.
CÆS.   You shall advise me in all for Cleopatra.
CLEO.   This is the brief[17] of money, plate and jewels,
    I am possess'd of: 'tis exactly valued,
    Not petty things admitted. Where's Seleucus?
SEL.   Here, madam.
CLEO.   This is my treasurer: let him speak, my lord,

16. *extenuate . . . enforce*] underrate . . . lay stress upon.
17. *brief*] inventory.

Upon his peril, that I have reserved
To myself nothing. Speak the truth, Seleucus.

SEL.　Madam,
I had rather seal my lips than to my peril
Speak that which is not.

CLEO.　　　　　　　　　　What have I kept back?

SEL.　Enough to purchase what you have made known.

CÆS.　Nay, blush not, Cleopatra; I approve
Your wisdom in the deed.

CLEO.　　　　　　　　　See, Cæsar! O, behold,
How pomp is follow'd! mine will now be yours,
And, should we shift estates, yours would be mine.
The ingratitude of this Seleucus does
Even make me wild. O slave, of no more trust
Than love that's hired! What, goest thou back? thou shalt
Go back, I warrant thee; but I'll catch thine eyes,
Though they had wings: slave, soulless villain, dog!
O rarely base!

CÆS.　　　　　　　Good queen, let us entreat you.

CLEO.　O Cæsar, what a wounding shame is this,
That thou vouchsafing here to visit me,
Doing the honour of thy lordliness
To one so meek, that mine own servant should
Parcel the sum of my disgraces by
Addition of his envy! Say, good Cæsar,
That I some lady trifles have reserved,
Immoment[18] toys, things of such dignity
As we greet modern[19] friends withal; and say,
Some nobler token I have kept apart
For Livia[20] and Octavia, to induce
Their mediation; must I be unfolded
With[21] one that I have bred? The gods! it smites me
Beneath the fall I have. [*To Seleucus*] Prithee, go hence;
Or I shall show the cinders of my spirits
Through the ashes of my chance:[22] wert thou a man,

---

18. *Immoment*] trifling, insignificant.
19. *modern*] commonplace, ordinary.
20. *Livia*] Livia Drusilla, wife of Cæsar.
21. *unfolded With*] exposed by.
22. *chance*] misfortunes.

       Thou wouldst have mercy on me.

CÆS.   Forbear, Seleucus.

                                         [Exit Seleucus.

CLEO.   Be it known, that we, the greatest, are misthought[23]
        For things that others do, and when we fall
        We answer others' merits in our name,[24]
        Are therefore to be pitied.

CÆS.   Cleopatra,
        Not what you have reserved, nor what acknowledged,
        Put we i' the roll of conquest: still be 't yours,
        Bestow it at your pleasure, and believe
        Cæsar's no merchant, to make prize with you
        Of things that merchants sold. Therefore be cheer'd;
        Make not your thoughts your prisons: no, dear queen;
        For we intend so to dispose you as
        Yourself shall give us counsel. Feed, and sleep:
        Our care and pity is so much upon you
        That we remain your friend; and so, adieu.

CLEO.   My master, and my lord!

CÆS.   Not so. Adieu.
                    [Flourish. Exeunt Cæsar and his train.

CLEO.   He words me, girls, he words me, that I should not
        Be noble to myself: but, hark thee, Charmian.
                        [Whispers Charmian.

IRAS.   Finish,[25] good lady; the bright day is done,
        And we are for the dark.

CLEO.   Hie thee again:
        I have spoke already, and it is provided;
        Go put it to the haste.

CHAR.   Madam, I will.

Re-enter DOLABELLA

DOL.   Where is the queen?

CHAR.   Behold, sir.   *[Exit.*

CLEO.   Dolabella!

DOL.   Madam, as thereto sworn by your command,
        Which my love makes religion to obey,

---

23. *misthought*] misjudged.
24. *We answer . . . name*] we are held accountable for the actions of others.
25. *Finish*] end, die.

I tell you this: Cæsar through Syria
Intends his journey, and within three days
You with your children will he send before:
Make your best use of this: I have perform'd
Your pleasure and my promise.

CLEO.   Dolabella,
I shall remain your debtor.

DOL.   I your servant.
Adieu, good queen; I must attend on Cæsar.

CLEO.   Farewell, and thanks.   [*Exit Dolabella.*
                              Now, Iras, what think'st thou?
Thou, an Egyptian puppet, shalt be shown
In Rome, as well as I: mechanic slaves
With greasy aprons, rules and hammers, shall
Uplift us to the view: in their thick breaths,
Rank of gross diet, shall we be enclouded
And forced to drink their vapour.

IRAS.   The gods forbid!

CLEO.   Nay, 'tis most certain, Iras: saucy lictors[26]
Will catch at us like strumpets, and scald[27] rhymers
Ballad us out o' tune: the quick[28] comedians
Extemporally will stage us and present
Our Alexandrian revels; Antony
Shall be brought drunken forth, and I shall see
Some squeaking Cleopatra boy my greatness[29]
I' the posture of a whore.

IRAS.   O the good gods!

CLEO.   Nay, that 's certain.

IRAS.   I 'll never see 't; for I am sure my nails
Are stronger than mine eyes.

CLEO.   Why, that 's the way
To fool their preparation, and to conquer
Their most absurd intents.

Re-enter CHARMIAN

26. *lictors*] the beadles of ancient Rome.
27. *scald*] scabby, scurvy.
28. *quick*] nimble, quick-witted.
29. *boy my greatness*] During Shakespeare's time, and up into the Restoration, women's parts were invariably acted by boys on stage.

Now, Charmian!
Show me, my women, like a queen: go fetch
My best attires: I am again for Cydnus,
To meet Mark Antony: sirrah Iras, go.
Now, noble Charmian, we 'll dispatch indeed,
And when thou hast done this chare I 'll give thee leave
To play till doomsday. Bring our crown and all.

> [*Exit Iras. A noise within.*

Wherefore 's this noise?

Enter a Guardsman

GUARD.   Here is a rural fellow
That will not be denied your highness' presence:
He brings you figs.
CLEO.   Let him come in.   [*Exit Guardsman.*
                    What poor an instrument
May do a noble deed! he brings me liberty.
My resolution 's placed, and I have nothing
Of woman in me: now from head to foot
I am marble-constant; now the fleeting[30] moon
No planet is of mine.

Re-enter Guardsman, *with* Clown *bringing in a basket*

GUARD.   This is the man.
CLEO.   Avoid,[31] and leave him.   [*Exit Guardsman.*
Hast thou the pretty worm[32] of Nilus there,
That kills and pains not?
CLOWN.   Truly, I have him: but I would not be the party that should
    desire you to touch him, for his biting is immortal;[33] those that do
    die of it do seldom or never recover.
CLEO.   Rememberest thou any that have died on 't?
CLOWN.   Very many, men and women too. I heard of one of them no
    longer than yesterday: a very honest woman, but something given
    to lie; as a woman should not do, but in the way of honesty: how
    she died of the biting of it, what pain she felt: truly, she makes a
    very good report o' the worm; but he that will believe all that they

---

30. *fleeting*] inconstant, changing.
31. *Avoid*] retire.
32. *worm*] asp or small venomous serpent.
33. *immortal*] blunder for "mortal," deadly.

say, shall never be saved by half that they do: but this is most fallible,[34] the worm's an odd worm.

CLEO.   Get thee hence; farewell.

CLOWN.   I wish you all joy of the worm.   [*Setting down his basket.*

CLEO.   Farewell.

CLOWN.   You must think this, look you, that the worm will do his
kind.[35]

CLEO.   Ay, ay; farewell.

CLOWN.   Look you, the worm is not to be trusted but in the keeping
of wise people, for indeed there is no goodness in the worm.

CLEO.   Take thou no care; it shall be heeded.

CLOWN.   Very good. Give it nothing, I pray you, for it is not worth the
feeding.

CLEO.   Will it eat me?

CLOWN.   You must not think I am so simple but I know the devil himself will not eat a woman: I know that a woman is a dish for the
gods, if the devil dress her not. But, truly, these same whoreson
devils do the gods great harm in their women; for in every ten that
they make, the devils mar five.

CLEO.   Well, get thee gone; farewell.

CLOWN.   Yes, forsooth: I wish you joy o' the worm.   [*Exit.*

Re-enter IRAS *with a robe, crown, &c.*

CLEO.   Give me my robe, put on my crown; I have
Immortal longings in me: now no more
The juice of Egypt's grape shall moist this lip:
Yare, yare, good Iras; quick. Methinks I hear
Antony call; I see him rouse himself
To praise my noble act; I hear him mock
The luck of Cæsar, which the gods give men
To excuse their after wrath. Husband, I come:
Now to that name my courage prove my title!
I am fire and air; my other elements
I give to baser life. So; have you done?
Come then and take the last warmth of my lips.
Farewell, kind Charmian; Iras, long farewell.
                    [*Kisses them. Iras falls and dies.*

34. *fallible*] blunder for "infallible," certain.
35. *do his kind*] act according to his nature.

Have I the aspic[36] in my lips? Dost fall?
If thou and nature can so gently part,
The stroke of death is as a lover's pinch,
Which hurts, and is desired. Dost thou lie still?
If thus thou vanishest, thou tell'st the world
It is not worth leave-taking.
CHAR.   Dissolve, thick cloud, and rain, that I may say
The gods themselves do weep!
CLEO.   This proves me base:
If she first meet the curled[37] Antony,
He 'll make demand of her, and spend that kiss
Which is my heaven to have. Come, thou mortal wretch,
                    [To an asp, which she applies to her breast.
With thy sharp teeth this knot intrinsicate[38]
Of life at once untie: poor venomous fool,
Be angry, and dispatch. O, couldst thou speak,
That I might hear thee call great Cæsar ass
Unpolicied![39]
CHAR.   O eastern star!
CLEO.   Peace, peace!
Dost thou not see my baby at my breast,
That sucks the nurse asleep?
CHAR.   O, break! O, break!
CLEO.   As sweet as balm, as soft as air, as gentle, —
O Antony! — Nay, I will take thee too:
                    [Applying another asp to her arm.
What[40] should I stay—   [Dies.
CHAR.   In this vile world? So, fare thee well.
Now boast thee, death, in thy possession lies
A lass unparallel'd. Downy windows,[41] close;
And golden Phœbus never be beheld
Of eyes again so royal! Your crown 's awry;
I 'll mend it, and then play.

Enter the Guard, rushing in

36. *aspic*] asp.
37. *curled*] well kempt.
38. *intrinsicate*] tightly drawn.
39. *Unpolicied*] outwitted.
40. *What*] why.
41. *Downy windows*] eyelids with their soft hair.

FIRST GUARD.   Where is the queen?
CHAR.   Speak softly, wake her not.
FIRST. GUARD.   Cæsar hath sent—
CHAR.   Too slow a messenger.
                                      [Applies an asp.

    O, come apace, dispatch: I partly feel thee.
FIRST GUARD.   Approach, ho! All's not well: Cæsar's beguiled.
SEC. GUARD.   There's Dolabella sent from Cæsar; call him.
FIRST GUARD.   What work is here! Charmian, is this well done?
CHAR.   It is well done, and fitting for a princess
    Descended of so many royal kings.
    Ah, soldier! -   *[Dies.*

Re-enter DOLABELLA

DOL.   How goes it here?
SEC. GUARD.   All dead.
DOL.   Cæsar, thy thoughts
    Touch their effects in this: thyself art coming
    To see perform'd the dreaded act which thou
    So sought'st to hinder.   [*Within.* "A way there, a way for Cæsar!"

Re-enter CÆSAR *and his train*

DOL.   O sir, you are too sure an augurer;
    That you did fear is done.
CÆS.   Bravest at the last,
    She levell'd[42] at our purposes, and being royal
    Took her own way. The manner of their deaths?
    I do not see them bleed.
DOL.   Who was last with them?
FIRST GUARD.   A simple countryman, that brought her figs:
    This was his basket.
CÆS.   Poison'd then.
FIRST GUARD.   O Cæsar,
    This Charmian lived but now; she stood and spake:
    I found her trimming up the diadem
    On her dead mistress; tremblingly she stood,
    And on the sudden dropp'd.
CÆS.   O noble weakness!
    If they had swallow'd poison, 't would appear

---

42. *levell'd*] guessed.

    By external swelling: but she looks like sleep,
    As she would catch another Antony
    In her strong toil of grace.
DOL.   Here, on her breast,
    There is a vent of blood, and something blown:[43]
    The like is on her arm.
FIRST GUARD.   This is an aspic's trail: and these fig-leaves
    Have slime upon them, such as the aspic leaves
    Upon the caves of Nile.
CÆS.   Most probable
    That so she died; for her physician tells me
    She hath pursued conclusions[44] infinite
    Of easy ways to die. Take up her bed,
    And bear her women from the monument:
    She shall be buried by her Antony:
    No grave upon the earth shall clip[45] in it
    A pair so famous. High events as these
    Strike those that make them; and their story is
    No less in pity than his glory which
    Brought them to be lamented. Our army shall
    In solemn show attend this funeral,
    And then to Rome. Come, Dolabella, see
    High order in this great solemnity.   [*Exeunt.*

43. *something blown*] somewhat swollen.
44. *conclusions*] experiments.
45. *clip*] embrace, enfold.

DOVER·THRIFT·EDITIONS

All books complete and unabridged. All 5³⁄₁₆ x 8¹⁄₄, paperbound.
Just $1.00—$2.00 in U.S.A.

A selection of the more than 200 titles in the series.

POETRY

DOVER BEACH AND OTHER POEMS, Matthew Arnold. 112pp. 28037-3 $1.00

BHAGAVADGITA, Bhagavadgita. 112pp. 27782-8 $1.00

SONGS OF INNOCENCE AND SONGS OF EXPERIENCE, William Blake. 64pp. 27051-3 $1.00

THE CLASSIC TRADITION OF HAIKU: An Anthology, Faubion Bowers (ed.). 96pp. 29274-6 $1.50

SONNETS FROM THE PORTUGUESE AND OTHER POEMS, Elizabeth Barrett Browning. 64pp. 27052-1 $1.00

MY LAST DUCHESS AND OTHER POEMS, Robert Browning. 128pp. 27783-6 $1.00

POEMS AND SONGS, Robert Burns. 96pp. 26863-2 $1.00

SELECTED POEMS, George Gordon, Lord Byron. 112pp. 27784-4 $1.00

THE RIME OF THE ANCIENT MARINER AND OTHER POEMS, Samuel Taylor Coleridge. 80pp. 27266-4 $1.00

SELECTED POEMS, Emily Dickinson. 64pp. 26466-1 $1.00

SELECTED POEMS, John Donne. 96pp. 27788-7 $1.00

THE RUBÁIYÁT OF OMAR KHAYYÁM: FIRST AND FIFTH EDITIONS, Edward FitzGerald. 64pp. 26467-X $1.00

A BOY'S WILL AND NORTH OF BOSTON, Robert Frost. 112pp. (Available in U.S. only) 26866-7 $1.00

THE ROAD NOT TAKEN AND OTHER POEMS, Robert Frost. 64pp. (Available in U.S. only) 27550-7 $1.00

A SHROPSHIRE LAD, A. E. Housman. 64pp. 26468-8 $1.00

LYRIC POEMS, John Keats. 80pp. 26871-3 $1.00

THE BOOK OF PSALMS, King James Bible. 128pp. 27541-8 $1.00

GUNGA DIN AND OTHER FAVORITE POEMS, Rudyard Kipling. 80pp. 26471-8 $1.00

THE CONGO AND OTHER POEMS, Vachel Lindsay. 96pp. 27272-9 $1.00

FAVORITE POEMS, Henry Wadsworth Longfellow. 96pp. 27273-7 $1.00

SPOON RIVER ANTHOLOGY, Edgar Lee Masters. 144pp. 27275-3 $1.00

RENASCENCE AND OTHER POEMS, Edna St. Vincent Millay. 64pp. (Available in U.S. only) 26873-X $1.00

SELECTED POEMS, John Milton. 128pp. 27554-X $1.00

GREAT SONNETS, Paul Negri (ed.). 96pp. 28052-7 $1.00

THE RAVEN AND OTHER FAVORITE POEMS, Edgar Allan Poe. 64pp. 26685-0 $1.00

ESSAY ON MAN AND OTHER POEMS, Alexander Pope. 128pp. 28053-5 $1.00

GOBLIN MARKET AND OTHER POEMS, Christina Rossetti. 64pp. 28055-1 $1.00

CHICAGO POEMS, Carl Sandburg. 80pp. 28057-8 $1.00

THE SHOOTING OF DAN McGREW AND OTHER POEMS, Robert Service. 96pp. 27556-6 $1.00

COMPLETE SONGS FROM THE PLAYS, William Shakespeare. 80pp. 27801-8 $1.00

COMPLETE SONNETS, William Shakespeare. 80pp. 26686-9 $1.00

SELECTED POEMS, Percy Bysshe Shelley. 128pp. 27558-2 $1.00

100 BEST-LOVED POEMS, Philip Smith (ed.). 96pp. 28553-7 $1.00

NATIVE AMERICAN SONGS AND POEMS: An Anthology, Brian Swann (ed.). 64pp. 29450-1 $1.00

SELECTED POEMS, Alfred Lord Tennyson. 112pp. 27282-6 $1.00

CHRISTMAS CAROLS: COMPLETE VERSES, Shane Weller (ed.). 64pp. 27397-0 $1.00

DOVER·THRIFT·EDITIONS

All books complete and unabridged. All 5³⁄₁₆ x 8¹⁄₄, paperbound.
Just $1.00—$2.00 in U.S.A.

GREAT LOVE POEMS, Shane Weller (ed.). 128pp. 27284-2 $1.00
SELECTED POEMS, Walt Whitman. 128pp. 26878-0 $1.00
THE BALLAD OF READING GAOL AND OTHER POEMS, Oscar Wilde. 64pp. 27072-6 $1.00
FAVORITE POEMS, William Wordsworth. 80pp. 27073-4 $1.00
EARLY POEMS, William Butler Yeats. 128pp. 27808-5 $1.00

FICTION

FLATLAND: A ROMANCE OF MANY DIMENSIONS, Edwin A. Abbott. 96pp. 27263-X $1.00
PERSUASION, Jane Austen. 224pp. 29555-9 $2.00
PRIDE AND PREJUDICE, Jane Austen. 272pp. 28473-5 $2.00
SENSE AND SENSIBILITY, Jane Austen. 272pp. 29049-2 $2.00
BEOWULF, Beowulf (trans. by R. K. Gordon). 64pp. 27264-8 $1.00
CIVIL WAR STORIES, Ambrose Bierce. 128pp. 28038-1 $1.00
TARZAN OF THE APES, Edgar Rice Burroughs. 224pp. 29570-2 $2.00
ALICE'S ADVENTURES IN WONDERLAND, Lewis Carroll. 96pp. 27543-4 $1.00
O PIONEERS!, Willa Cather. 128pp. 27785-2 $1.00
FIVE GREAT SHORT STORIES, Anton Chekhov. 96pp. 26463-7 $1.00
FAVORITE FATHER BROWN STORIES, G. K. Chesterton. 96pp. 27545-0 $1.00
THE AWAKENING, Kate Chopin. 128pp. 27786-0 $1.00
HEART OF DARKNESS, Joseph Conrad. 80pp. 26464-5 $1.00
THE SECRET SHARER AND OTHER STORIES, Joseph Conrad. 128pp. 27546-9 $1.00
THE "LITTLE REGIMENT" AND OTHER CIVIL WAR STORIES, Stephen Crane. 80pp. 29557-5 $1.00
THE OPEN BOAT AND OTHER STORIES, Stephen Crane. 128pp. 27547-7 $1.00
THE RED BADGE OF COURAGE, Stephen Crane. 112pp. 26465-3 $1.00
A CHRISTMAS CAROL, Charles Dickens. 80pp. 26865-9 $1.00
THE CRICKET ON THE HEARTH AND OTHER CHRISTMAS STORIES, Charles Dickens. 128pp.
    28039-X $1.00
THE DOUBLE, Fyodor Dostoyevsky. 128pp. 29572-9 $1.50
NOTES FROM THE UNDERGROUND, Fyodor Dostoyevsky. 96pp. 27053-X $1.00
THE ADVENTURE OF THE DANCING MEN AND OTHER STORIES, Sir Arthur Conan Doyle.
    80pp. 29558-3 $1.00
SIX GREAT SHERLOCK HOLMES STORIES, Sir Arthur Conan Doyle. 112pp. 27055-6 $1.00
SILAS MARNER, George Eliot. 160pp. 29246-0 $1.50
MADAME BOVARY, Gustave Flaubert. 256pp. 29257-6 $2.00
WHERE ANGELS FEAR TO TREAD, E. M. Forster. 128pp. (Available in U.S. only) 27791-7 $1.00
THE OVERCOAT AND OTHER STORIES, Nikolai Gogol. 112pp. 27057-2 $1.00
GREAT GHOST STORIES, John Grafton (ed.). 112pp. 27270-2 $1.00
THE MABINOGION, Lady Charlotte E. Guest. 192pp. 29541-9 $2.00
THE LUCK OF ROARING CAMP AND OTHER STORIES, Bret Harte. 96pp. 27271-0 $1.00
THE SCARLET LETTER, Nathaniel Hawthorne. 192pp. 28048-9 $2.00
YOUNG GOODMAN BROWN AND OTHER STORIES, Nathaniel Hawthorne. 128pp. 27060-2 $1.00
THE GIFT OF THE MAGI AND OTHER SHORT STORIES, O. Henry. 96pp. 27061-0 $1.00
THE NUTCRACKER AND THE GOLDEN POT, E. T. A. Hoffmann. 128pp. 27806-9 $1.00
THE BEAST IN THE JUNGLE AND OTHER STORIES, Henry James. 128pp. 27552-3 $1.00
THE TURN OF THE SCREW, Henry James. 96pp. 26684-2 $1.00

DOVER · THRIFT · EDITIONS

All books complete and unabridged. All 5³⁄₁₆ x 8¹⁄₄, paperbound.
Just $1.00—$2.00 in U.S.A.

DUBLINERS, James Joyce. 160pp. 26870-5 $1.00
A PORTRAIT OF THE ARTIST AS A YOUNG MAN, James Joyce. 192pp. 28050-0 $2.00
THE MAN WHO WOULD BE KING AND OTHER STORIES, Rudyard Kipling. 128pp. 28051-9 $1.00
SELECTED SHORT STORIES, D. H. Lawrence. 128pp. 27794-1 $1.00
GREEN TEA AND OTHER GHOST STORIES, J. Sheridan LeFanu. 96pp. 27795-X $1.00

THE CALL OF THE WILD, Jack London. 64pp. 26472-6 $1.00
FIVE GREAT SHORT STORIES, Jack London. 96pp. 27063-7 $1.00
WHITE FANG, Jack London. 160pp. 26968-X $1.00
THE NECKLACE AND OTHER SHORT STORIES, Guy de Maupassant. 128pp. 27064-5 $1.00
BARTLEBY AND BENITO CERENO, Herman Melville. 112pp. 26473-4 $1.00
THE GOLD-BUG AND OTHER TALES, Edgar Allan Poe. 128pp. 26875-6 $1.00
TALES OF TERROR AND DETECTION, Edgar Allan Poe. 96pp. 28744-0 $1.00
THE QUEEN OF SPADES AND OTHER STORIES, Alexander Pushkin. 128pp. 28054-3 $1.00
FRANKENSTEIN, Mary Shelley. 176pp. 28211-2 $1.00
THREE LIVES, Gertrude Stein. 176pp. 28059-4 $2.00
THE STRANGE CASE OF DR. JEKYLL AND MR. HYDE, Robert Louis Stevenson. 64pp. 26688-5 $1.00
TREASURE ISLAND, Robert Louis Stevenson. 160pp. 27559-0 $1.00
GULLIVER'S TRAVELS, Jonathan Swift. 240pp. 29273-8 $2.00
THE KREUTZER SONATA AND OTHER SHORT STORIES, Leo Tolstoy. 144pp. 27805-0 $1.00
ADVENTURES OF HUCKLEBERRY FINN, Mark Twain. 224pp. 28061-6 $2.00
THE MYSTERIOUS STRANGER AND OTHER STORIES, Mark Twain. 128pp. 27069-6 $1.00
CANDIDE, Voltaire (François-Marie Arouet). 112pp. 26689-3 $1.00
"THE COUNTRY OF THE BLIND" AND OTHER SCIENCE-FICTION STORIES, H. G. Wells. 160pp. (Available in U.S. only) 29569-9 $1.50
THE INVISIBLE MAN, H. G. Wells. 112pp. (Available in U.S. only) 27071-8 $1.00
THE WAR OF THE WORLDS, H. G. Wells. 160pp. (Available in U.S. only) 29506-0 $1.00
ETHAN FROME, Edith Wharton. 96pp. 26690-7 $1.00
THE PICTURE OF DORIAN GRAY, Oscar Wilde. 192pp. 27807-7 $1.00
MONDAY OR TUESDAY: Eight Stories, Virginia Woolf. 64pp. 29453-6 $1.00

NONFICTION

THE DEVIL'S DICTIONARY, Ambrose Bierce. 144pp. 27542-6 $1.00
THE SOULS OF BLACK FOLK, W. E. B. Du Bois. 176pp. 28041-1 $2.00
SELF-RELIANCE AND OTHER ESSAYS, Ralph Waldo Emerson. 128pp. 27790-9 $1.00
THE AUTOBIOGRAPHY OF BENJAMIN FRANKLIN, Benjamin Franklin. 144pp. 29073-5 $1.50
THE STORY OF MY LIFE, Helen Keller. 80pp. 29249-5 $1.00
GREAT SPEECHES, Abraham Lincoln. 112pp. 26872-1 $1.00
THE PRINCE, Niccolò Machiavelli. 80pp. 27274-5 $1.00
SYMPOSIUM AND PHAEDRUS, Plato. 96pp. 27798-4 $1.00
THE TRIAL AND DEATH OF SOCRATES: Four Dialogues, Plato. 128pp. 27066-1 $1.00
CIVIL DISOBEDIENCE AND OTHER ESSAYS, Henry David Thoreau. 96pp. 27563-9 $1.00
THE THEORY OF THE LEISURE CLASS, Thorstein Veblen. 256pp. 28062-4 $2.00

DOVER·THRIFT·EDITIONS

All books complete and unabridged. All 5³⁄₁₆ x 8¹⁄₄, paperbound.
Just $1.00—$2.00 in U.S.A.

PLAYS

PROMETHEUS BOUND, Aeschylus. 64pp. 28762-9 $1.00

WHAT EVERY WOMAN KNOWS, James Barrie. 80pp. 29578-8 $1.50

THE CHERRY ORCHARD, Anton Chekhov. 64pp. 26682-6 $1.00

THE THREE SISTERS, Anton Chekhov. 64pp. 27544-2 $1.00

THE WAY OF THE WORLD, William Congreve. 80pp. 27787-9 $1.00

BACCHAE, Euripides. 64pp. 29580-X $1.00

MEDEA, Euripides. 64pp. 27548-5 $1.00

THE MIKADO, William Schwenck Gilbert. 64pp. 27268-0 $1.00

FAUST, PART ONE, Johann Wolfgang von Goethe. 192pp. 28046-2 $2.00

SHE STOOPS TO CONQUER, Oliver Goldsmith. 80pp. 26867-5 $1.00

A DOLL'S HOUSE, Henrik Ibsen. 80pp. 27062-9 $1.00

HEDDA GABLER, Henrik Ibsen. 80pp. 26469-6 $1.00

VOLPONE, Ben Jonson. 112pp. 28049-7 $1.00

DR. FAUSTUS, Christopher Marlowe. 64pp. 28208-2 $1.00

THE MISANTHROPE, Molière. 64pp. 27065-3 $1.00

THE EMPEROR JONES, Eugene O'Neill. 64pp. 29268-1 $1.50

RIGHT YOU ARE, IF YOU THINK YOU ARE, Luigi Pirandello. 64pp. 29576-1 $1.50

HANDS AROUND, Arthur Schnitzler. 64pp. 28724-6 $1.00

HAMLET, William Shakespeare. 128pp. 27278-8 $1.00

HENRY IV, William Shakespeare. 96pp. 29584-2 $1.00

JULIUS CAESAR, William Shakespeare. 80pp. 26876-4 $1.00

KING LEAR, William Shakespeare. 112pp. 28058-6 $1.00

MACBETH, William Shakespeare. 96pp. 27802-6 $1.00

A MIDSUMMER NIGHT'S DREAM, William Shakespeare. 80pp. 27067-X $1.00

ROMEO AND JULIET, William Shakespeare. 96pp. 27557-4 $1.00

ARMS AND THE MAN, George Bernard Shaw. 80pp. (Available in U.S. only) 26476-9 $1.00

THE SCHOOL FOR SCANDAL, Richard Brinsley Sheridan. 96pp. 26687-7 $1.00

ANTIGONE, Sophocles. 64pp. 27804-2 $1.00

OEDIPUS REX, Sophocles. 64pp. 26877-2 $1.00

MISS JULIE, August Strindberg. 64pp. 27281-8 $1.00

THE PLAYBOY OF THE WESTERN WORLD AND RIDERS TO THE SEA, J. M. Synge. 80pp. 27562-0 $1.00

THE IMPORTANCE OF BEING EARNEST, Oscar Wilde. 64pp. 26478-5 $1.00

For a complete descriptive list of all volumes in the Dover Thrift Editions series
write for a free Dover Fiction and Literature Catalog (59047-X) to
Dover Publications, Inc., Dept. DTE, 31 E. 2nd Street, Mineola, N.Y. 11501